A HISTORY OF THE
ROYAL OPERA
HOUSE

COVENT GARDEN
1732-1982

A HISTORY OF THE
ROYAL OPERA
HOUSE
COVENT GARDEN
1732-1982

Andrew Saint

B.A. Young

Mary Clarke and Clement Crisp

Harold Rosenthal

The Royal Opera House

Publication sponsored by Commercial Union Assurance

The paper for this book has been donated by
Bunzl Pulp and Paper (Sales) Limited

Published by
The Royal Opera House
Covent Garden Limited, London WC2E 7QA

ISBN 0 946338 00 0 (Hardback)
ISBN 0 946338 01 9 (Paperback)

THE ROYAL OPERA HOUSE
IS SUBSIDISED BY THE Arts Council OF GREAT BRITAIN

Covent Garden's Three Theatres © 1982 Andrew Saint
From Playhouse to Opera House © 1982 B.A. Young
Dance at Covent Garden © 1982 Mary Clarke and Clement Crisp
Opera and Music at Covent Garden © 1982 Harold Rosenthal
Editorial material © 1982 Royal Opera House Covent Garden Limited
First published 1982

British Library Cataloguing in Publication Data

A History of the Royal Opera House: Covent Garden
1732-1982
1. Royal Opera House—History
I. Saint, Andrew   II. Royal Opera House
782.1'09421'32   PN2596.L7R/

Editors for the Royal Opera House, Covent Garden
Francesca Franchi and Henry Fryer

Designed and typeset by Logos Design
Printed in Great Britain by Jolly & Barber Limited

Contents

Foreword   6

Introduction   7

Covent Garden's Three Theatres   11

From Playhouse to Opera House   41

Dance at Covent Garden   63

Opera and Music at Covent Garden   91

Contributors   122

Acknowledgements   123

Index   124

Foreword

The 250th anniversary of the opening of a theatre by my predecessor, John Rich, gives us the chance to take stock of some of the things that have happened and continue to happen on this site in the heart of London.

On that distant day, 7 December 1732, it was not an opera or a ballet that was presented but *The Way of the World* by William Congreve, soon to be followed by *The Beggar's Opera* by John Gay. Thus the first production was a play and the second a 'musical' and this sets the scene for the future life of this theatre.

It is true that it was not long before opera was to be heard and it is appropriate that on 7 December 1982 there will be a performance of Handel's *Semele*, first seen here at its premiere in 1744. Ballet, if not in the form in which we know it today, joined the repertory before long, though it is difficult to give a precise date.

Covent Garden has always been a theatre 'for all seasons' and over the years has been host to every form of theatrical venture not excluding pantomime, circus, skating and ballroom dancing.

Fire was the great enemy of the theatre in the eighteenth and nineteenth centuries which is hardly surprising when the only lighting was by candle and oil lamp. We did not escape this fate of being burned down in 1808 and 1856. That the theatre was always rebuilt immediately says something for its popularity, and the present building dating from 1858 has constantly been adapted and renovated, a fact amply demonstrated by the splendid new extension recently opened by the Patron of The Royal Opera, His Royal Highness, The Prince of Wales.

After a wartime period as a *palais de danse*, showing its continuing ability to adapt to the conditions of the day, the theatre re-opened in 1946 with a performance of *The Sleeping Beauty* shortly to be followed by regular evenings of opera. Since then the House has settled into a regular pattern of performing ballet and opera with occasional excursions into concert and recital. Today the theatre is shared equally between The Royal Ballet and The Royal Opera.

It has had many names, but one remains second to none. Whether it has technically been the Theatre Royal or the Royal Opera House it has always popularly and affectionately been called Covent Garden. I like to think that these two emotive words, as with Rolls Royce, have about them the ring of excellence, for it is our aim to provide opera and ballet at their highest possible level and offer the public all that is best the world over.

One golden thread links us with our past and that is the tradition of entertainment, in the best possible sense of the word, and I hope that this book may bear this out by celebrating in words and pictures two and a half centuries in the life of a famous and much loved theatre.

Sir John Tooley
General Director

Introduction

The Royal Opera House in its present form is so familiar to opera and ballet lovers the world over that it is sometimes difficult to imagine that it was ever different. Yet not only is the present theatre the third of three very different buildings to stand upon the site, but its role as an opera house extends over only slightly more than half its 250 year history. Furthermore, the present arrangement of resident opera and ballet companies sharing a season from approximately September to July dates back a mere thirty-six years. The anniversary of the opening of the first theatre in 1732 provides the opportunity of examining the history of the three different theatres, and the entertainments which they have housed, over this 250 year span. This book looks at the theatre's history from four viewpoints – architecture, drama, dance and opera.

The theatre's history really begins not with its foundation in 1732, but in 1662, with the granting by Charles II of two sets of Letters Patent which allowed their owners sole rights to build theatres and produce drama in the capital. It was one of these two sets of Patents, granted

to Sir William Davenant, that eventually came down to John Rich, actor, harlequin, and Manager of the theatre at Lincoln's Inn Fields, and it was the immense success of his production of *The Beggar's Opera* that provided Rich with the capital to commission Edward Shepherd to build a new and larger theatre at Covent Garden. Andrew Saint's opening contribution describes in detail the arrangements surrounding the building of the three theatres, their decorations, alterations and some of their managers.

For the first hundred years or so, the Theatre Royal, Covent Garden, was a playhouse, offering its patrons a rich and varied fare. The second set of Patents had led to the building of the Theatre Royal, Drury Lane, and the two Patent theatres were in constant competition, with managers borrowing – by fair means or foul – players and ideas from one another. Few of the great players of the eighteenth and early nineteenth centuries appeared at one Theatre Royal without at some time appearing at the other. Plays and pantomimes, dancing, musical interludes and farces alternated with musical

1 *Rich's Glory*, by William Hogarth: John Rich's triumphant entry to Covent Garden for the opening of his new Theatre Royal, 7 December 1732

pieces, operas and oratorios, and audience reaction was decisive not only in ensuring the success or otherwise of a production, but also in dictating the way in which the theatre was managed. Attempts by the management to introduce price rises often met with considerable opposition – the most violent reaction being in 1809 when the OP (Old Prices) Riots continued for over two months. These price riots – one of the most celebrated events in British theatrical history – followed the opening of the second theatre, replacing the first which had been destroyed by fire in 1808. Built in less than a year, and in grander style, its cost was so great that the management attempted to recoup some of their costs with increased prices. As a result, performances were interrupted, the

building's fabric threatened, and they had no option but to give way.

For the next thirty-five years, the theatre continued as a playhouse, but following the huge costs of rebuilding, successive managements found it increasingly difficult to make ends meet, and when the Theatres' Act of 1843 ended the monopoly of the two Patent Theatres, it also effectively ended Covent Garden's role as one of the leading drama houses in London. It is the period from 1732 to 1847, and subsequent scattered 'dramatic' events at Covent Garden, that are described in the second section by B.A. Young.

The third section covers dance at Covent Garden, which has played a continuous, but not always prominent, role in this theatre. Mary Clarke and Clement Crisp describe the stars of the eighteenth and nineteenth centuries who shine out from the dance events of those years, through the important seasons of the Russian Ballet in the early twentieth century to the eventual settling of our national ballet at Covent Garden after the Second World War.

By the mid-nineteenth century, when Covent Garden's fortunes had reached their lowest ebb, Her Majesty's Theatre in the Haymarket had been the main home of opera and ballet in London for over a hundred years. In 1846, following a disagreement with the management of Her Majesty's, Michael Costa, its Conductor and Music Director, moved to Covent Garden bringing with him most of his company of singers. In partnership with Frederick Beale and others he arranged for the reconstruction of the theatre's interior, and, on 6 April 1847, the Royal Italian Opera, Covent Garden opened with a performance of *Semiramide*. It is here that the final section of our history, by Harold Rosenthal, has its true beginning – although the operas, oratorios and other musical events that had formed part of the seasons under the management of John Rich and his successors are also described.

At Covent Garden, performances of opera by Italian composers now alternated with works translated into Italian, in short seasons from April to August, with an occasional winter season. Between these, the theatre remained closed unless some enterprising impresario hired it to present circuses, concerts or masked balls – and it was after one such *bal masqué* at the end of a season presented by Professor J.H. Anderson, the self-styled 'Wizard of the North', that the second theatre was destroyed by fire in 1856.

Financial constraints delayed rebuilding until 1857, when it progressed with extraordinary speed, and the builders were barely off the site before the doors opened on 15 May 1858 for a

2 Programmes at the Theatre Royal, Covent Garden in the eighteenth century generally offered a number of items of diverse character, including songs and dancing as well as drama: one of the earliest surviving playbills, 15 January 1755

Acted but Twice these Twelve Years.

AT THE

THEATRE ROYAL in *Covent-Garden*,

This present *Wednesday*, being the 15th of *January*,

Will be Reviv'd the TRAGEDY of

OEDIPUS,

KING of THEBES.

The Part of OEDIPUS to be perform'd

By Mr SHERIDAN,

Creon by Mr. SPARKS,

Phorbas by Mr. RYAN,

Ægeon by Mr. RIDOUT,

Tiresias by Mr. GIBSON,

Manto (with a Song in Character) by Mrs. CHAMBERS,

Alcander by Mr. CUSHING, Ghost of Laius, Mr. ANDERSON,

Hæmon by Mr. WHITE, Pyracmon by Mr. REDMAN,

Adrastus by Mr. SMITH,

Eurydice by Mrs. VINCENT,

And the Part of JOCASTA to be perform'd

By Mrs WOFFINGTON,

With all Proper DECORATIONS.

With a Comic Entertainment of Dancing.

TO BE PERFORM'D

By Mr. POITIER, Junior.

AND

Mademoiselle CAPDEVILLE.

To which will be added a FARCE, call'd

The CHEATS of SCAPIN.

Scapin by Mr. SHUTER.

Boxes 5 s.　Pit 3 s.　First Gallery 2 s.　Upper Gallery 1 s.

To-morrow, HAMLET.

3 The production of *The Sleeping Beauty* which reopened the Royal Opera House after the Second World War on 20 February 1946, in the presence of members of the Royal Family

performance of *Les Huguenots*. The theatre continued to be known as the Royal Italian Opera until 1892, when 'Italian' was dropped from the title as the number of French and German works given in their original languages increased. This was a golden age of opera at Covent Garden with such stars as Patti, Melba, Caruso and the de Reszke brothers.

After closure during the First World War, short opera seasons resumed under the management of Thomas Beecham, interspersed with a variety of entertainments, including ballroom dancing, circuses, film shows, cabarets and the traditional Covent Garden pantomimes. These continued up to the outbreak of the

Second World War, during which the theatre was leased to Mecca Cafés for use as a dance hall for the troops. And it might have remained such after the War but for the initiative of Leslie Boosey and Ralph Hawkes, the music publishers, who acquired the lease of the building, setting it on its course towards becoming a national home for opera and ballet.

David Webster was appointed General Administrator and Ninette de Valois was invited to give her Sadler's Wells Ballet Company a home at Covent Garden, and it was they who reopened the Opera House on 20 February 1946 with a sumptuous production of *The Sleeping Beauty*. David Webster and his Music Director

4 After the reconstruction of the interior of the second Theatre Royal, Covent Garden by Benedict Albano, it reopened as the Royal Italian Opera on 6 April 1847 with a performance of Rossini's *Semiramide*, with Giulia Grisi in the title role

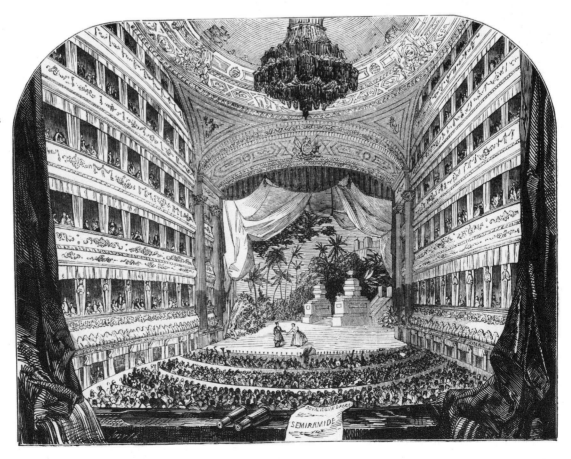

Karl Rankl immediately began working to build a resident Opera Company, and in December 1946 the Ballet and Opera Companies gave a joint production of *The Fairy Queen*. On 14 January 1947 the Covent Garden Opera Company gave its first performance with *Carmen*. Since then the Ballet and Opera Companies have shared joint seasons at the Opera House and were granted Royal charters in 1956 and 1968 respectively.

This, then, is a short history of the present theatre at Covent Garden, which in 1982 celebrates its 250th anniversary. No book of this scope can hope to do more than convey the flavour of such a rich and varied period, and it is inevitable that some readers will be disappointed by omissions which limitations of space have forced on us. Nonetheless, we hope that all will find some aspect of the theatre's past which can both surprise and please them in the pages which follow.

5 The Royal Opera House, Covent Garden as it is today: the theatre, designed by E.M. Barry, 1857-8, is the third to stand on the site

Covent Garden's Three Theatres

ANDREW SAINT

The First Theatre 1732-1808

'We hear the Subscription for building a new Theatre in Bow-street, Covent-Garden, for Mr Rich, amounts to upward of £6,000, and that the same will be very speedily begun by that ingenious Architect James Sheppard, Esq'; so announced *The Daily Courant* early in 1731.[1] Eighteenth-century journalism was notoriously inaccurate. In fact, subscriptions for the theatre had yet to be openly solicited, and the intended architect's true name was Edward Shepherd. Nevertheless the *Courant* had scored a coup in breaking to the public the news of the great project for the first Theatre Royal, Covent Garden, ancestor of the Royal Opera House and the earliest of three celebrated theatres to rise upon the present site.

The history of the first Covent Garden theatre is rooted in the complex tangle which enmeshed the 'legitimate' London theatre in the late seventeenth century. After the suppression of theatres under the Commonwealth, Charles II at his restoration granted two fresh royal 'Patents' for the exclusive rights of building and managing theatres in London and Westminster. One was issued to Thomas Killigrew, a courtier and minor playwright; the other was renewed rather than granted to the Poet Laureate and veteran dramatist Sir William Davenant. Eventually, after many complicated transfers and divisions, Killigrew's Patent descended to the Theatre Royal, Drury Lane, and Davenant's to the Theatre Royal, Covent Garden. The two theatres bore their titles on the strength of their royal Patents, and were in theory the only recognized playhouses in central London until 1843. In practice, their monopoly became less of a reality during the eighteenth century, as new theatres sprang up under licences of one kind or another.

The immediate predecessor to the Covent Garden Theatre lay in Portugal Street, off Lincoln's Inn Fields. This theatre, converted from an old tennis court by Davenant for the use of his actors in about 1660-1, came after many vicissitudes into the hands of Christopher Rich, 'an attorney of inexhaustible guile'[2], and hence at his death in 1714 to his son John Rich,

1 *The Daily Courant*, 12 January 1730/1
2 F.H.W. Sheppard in *Survey of London*, vol XXXV, 1970, p3

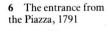

6 The entrance from the Piazza, 1791

promoter, first actor-manager of the Covent Garden Theatre and the man with the best claim to be the inventor of English pantomime. It was the huge success of John Gay's *The Beggar's Opera*, first staged in 1728 at Lincoln's Inn Fields and constantly repeated, that prompted Rich to build a larger theatre elsewhere.

The land where Rich proposed to build his new and bigger theatre was not in 1731-2 a virgin site. It belonged to the Dukes of Bedford, who continued to own the freehold of the successive theatres until 1918. Close by, the fourth Earl of Bedford had in the 1630s promoted the renowned Covent Garden Piazza, designed by Inigo Jones with St Paul's Church at the west end and an arcade along its north and east sides. A century later, the Piazza was already in social decline, as the district became densely built up and a flourishing market began to strangle the centre of the square. The land which the Bedfords leased to Rich included several houses in the north-east corner of the Piazza, behind which lay a medley of houses and stables stretching northwards up to Hart Street (now Floral Street) and with a shorter frontage facing Bow Street. These last buildings Rich undertook to demolish in order to erect his 'new Grand Theatre'.

Externally the new building had no chance to be grand at all, for like many early theatres it was hemmed in by other buildings and approached down alleys. The better patrons who took the boxes came through an ornate double-door (ridiculed by the architect William Kent as 'an Ionick expencive portico'[3]) set at the back of the arcade in the north-east angle of the Piazza. Those destined for the pit or the galleries proceeded along a short passage from Bow Street, while towards Hart Street was the stage entrance.

The interior of the theatre was of greater consequence, but probably not especially original. The arrangement of most early Georgian theatres in England can be traced back to two buildings: the second Drury Lane Theatre, designed probably by Sir Christopher Wren in 1674, and the Haymarket Opera House, built by the playwright-turned-architect Sir John Vanbrugh in 1704-5. In 1731 both Wren and Vanbrugh were dead; Rich's choice fell upon the architect and builder Edward Shepherd, a figure well enough known in his day. Shepherd was particularly involved with high-class speculative development in Mayfair, where Shepherd Market perpetuates his name. He was also the architect who completed the great mansion of Cannons for the Duke of Chandos, an enthusiast for the theatre, an important patron of Handel, and one of the original subscribers to Covent Garden. While building Covent Garden, Shepherd also built a smaller theatre at Goodman's Fields, Whitechapel.

7   Scale recon-
struction of the first
Theatre Royal, Covent
Garden drawn by
Richard Leacroft

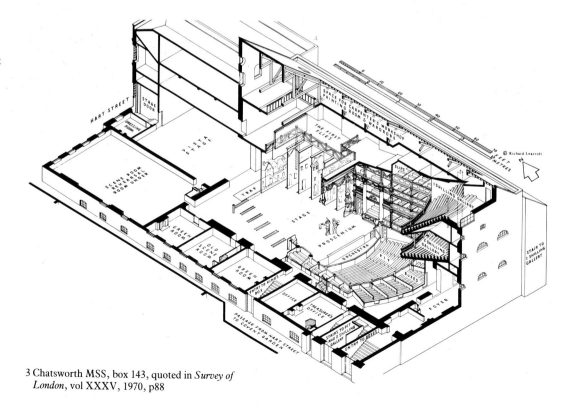

3 Chatsworth MSS, box 143, quoted in *Survey of London*, vol XXXV, 1970, p88

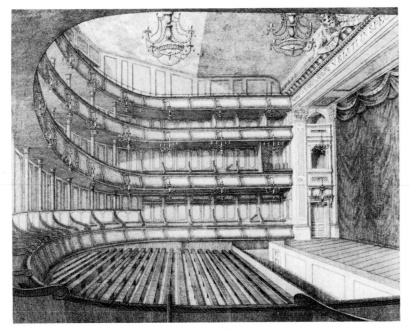

Edward Shepherd had been a plasterer before he became an architect, and customarily used plaster or stucco in all his buildings instead of the more usual panelling and external stonework. Since plaster is safer than panelling in case of fire, and fires were a notorious cause of destruction in theatres, this may be why Shepherd's manner of building appealed to Rich. As another measure of safety, iron was concealed within the interior supports of the galleries; in 1763, during the first of several price-riots at the theatre, the rioters 'cut away the wooden pillars between the boxes, so if the inside of them had not been iron, they would have brought down the galleries on their heads'[4].

According to one press report, the new theatre was based upon the Haymarket Opera House. But the agreement signed between Rich and Shepherd suggests that a likelier model was the theatre at Lincoln's Inn Fields, which in turn was apparently rebuilt by Rich's father on the lines of Wren's second Drury Lane Theatre.

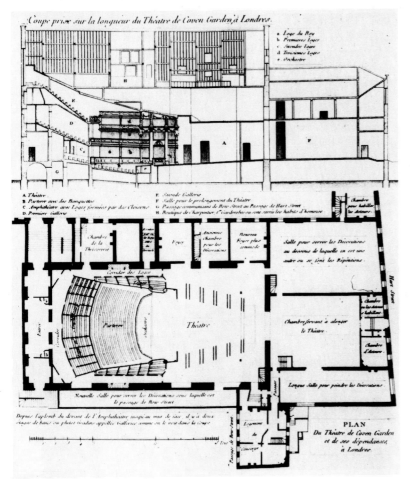

8   Interior of the first Theatre Royal, Covent Garden showing Henry Holland's alterations of 1792

9   Plan of Edward Shepherd's theatre of 1732, engraved c.1774

10 View from the front boxes of Covent Garden Theatre, c.1770

4 J.C. Whitty in *Theatre Notebook*, vol. 24, pp 25-32

11 The auditorium in 1786 from an engraving by Thomas Rowlandson, 1786

12 The auditorium during a performance of an Oratorio, drawing by A. Van Assen, c.1800

The distinctive feature of all these theatres was a fan-shaped auditorium which tapered towards the stage. To modern eyes this is a curious arrangement, since those who sat in the side boxes were at an oblique angle to the stage. But at this period, most of the acting took place on an apron set forward of the proscenium, so the sight-lines from these seats were not seriously impeded. Besides, since illumination remained 'up' in the house during the performances, eighteenth-century audiences went to the theatre as much to be seen as to see. Shepherd's small, fan-shaped auditorium approximated to a rectangle, in which the side boxes were only some thirty feet away from each other across the pit and the galleries began roughly the same distance from the front of the apron, so these needs were well catered for.

The arrangement of the seating was simple. There were twelve rows of hard, backless benches in the pit, three tiers of boxes at the sides, and two deep galleries at the back. Behind the pit, the amphitheatre was divided into nine capacious boxes, of which the largest was the 'King's Front Box': these were the best seats in the house. Alternatively, royalty could use one of two boxes set on either side of the apron front. Here, left and right of the proscenium, the decoration broke out into pilastered grandeur at odds with the simplicity that prevailed in the main auditorium. The ceiling, which was raked back steeply from the proscenium, was also generally plain, but over the apron was a painting by Jacopo Amiconi of Apollo and the Muses awarding the laurel to Shakespeare.

The proscenium arch itself was neither deep nor high. Behind it, the back stage originally extended only about thirty feet to a painted backdrop, with the customary wing scenery set in grooves and protruding slightly on either

side. But by 1760 Rich had rebuilt the houses facing Hart Street so as to form a generous 'vista stage' behind the main stage, with 'tiring rooms' for changing and others for rehearsal nearby.

Though Shepherd managed to quarrel with Rich while the theatre was being built, in due course he received the full amount of the contract price, £5,600, plus £50 for extras. By this time the theatre had been functioning for two years, having opened with Congreve's *The Way of the World* in December 1732. Artistically the most important events of these early years were the series of Handel opera premieres given in 1735-7. So costly did these prove that Rich had to postpone paying his rent to the Duke of Bedford, adducing 'Severe Losses by the Operas etc carryd by Mr Handel and my Self at Covent Garden Theatre for these three years last past'[5]. Thereafter he reverted to a mixed diet of plays, oratorios, opera and pantomime which suited the public appetite better; under this arrangement Covent Garden prospered.

5 Greater London Record Office, Bedford Estate Papers, E/BER/CG/E8/10/1

The twenty years after Rich's death in 1761 were more turbulent. The day-to-day running of the theatre passed first to his son-in-law John Beard, and then to a partnership which included the dramatist George Colman the elder and Thomas Harris. Though never an actor, Harris became the pre-eminent figure in the theatre's history for many years. Shortly after he gained overall control, Harris in 1782 set about improving the theatre which, it was now believed, had been built 'on erroneous principles'[6] – a reference to the fan-shaped auditorium. For this task Harris turned to John Inigo Richards, then scene-painter at the theatre. Richards straightened the sides of the auditorium, gave it a flat ceiling painted with clouds and made other major alterations.

This arrangement was superseded by a more fundamental reconstruction, undertaken during a blitz of theatre-building which struck London between 1789 and 1794. First, the old Haymarket Theatre burned down in 1789 and gave way to a grand opera house designed by Michael Novosielski. This spurred on Sheridan, then managing Drury Lane, to raise the handsomest theatre yet built in London, designed by Henry Holland, the most accomplished English architect of his generation. Holland's Drury Lane Theatre was conceived in 1791 but not finished until 1794. Meanwhile, during 1791 Thomas Harris, not to be outdone by Sheridan, also brought in Holland to reconstruct the Covent Garden auditorium. The task was completed in the summer of 1792 and the theatre re-opened on 17 September; so Harris had pipped Sheridan to the post, having spent just £30,000 as against nearly £80,000 lavished on rebuilding Drury Lane.

The general appearance of Holland's Drury Lane and Covent Garden theatres was similar: out went the three-sided auditorium, and in came horseshoe-shaped tiers resting on cast-iron columns, in the fashion of recent French theatre architecture. But Covent Garden remained comparatively informal and intimate; its seating hardly increased and the theatre itself was still hemmed in behind the houses of Hart Street and Bow Street. A simple projecting portico dignified the entrance from Bow Street, which became the main means of approach. Westwards of the stage, Holland also added a neat building facing Hart Street including a new 'King's Entrance'. As for the finishings of the interior, these were mostly (for acoustical reasons) of painted but unpapered board. 'That the sound may have an uninterrupted circulation, neither cloth, silk, nor linen, is used in decorating the Boxes, and water colour is used instead of oil paint', noted *The World*.[7] The colours were those that were to become traditional to the theatre – pearl-white and red with gilt ornament.

Henry Holland's Drury Lane and Covent Garden, having been built almost together, were to perish almost together. On the morning of 20 September 1808 Covent Garden Theatre, with all the buildings round it, burned to the ground. No one was sure of the cause, but one idea was that hot wadding from a gun fired during a rendering of Sheridan's *Pizarro* the previous evening had got caught in the scenery and smouldered through the night. Five months later, a similar fate befell Drury Lane. The great theatre subsequently raised on the site of Drury Lane survives to this day. Covent Garden, on the other hand, had yet to undergo one further trial by fire before arriving at its present form.

The Second Theatre 1809-56

At the time of the fire of 1808, Thomas Harris was still in charge at the Theatre Royal, Covent Garden, by now in collaboration with John Philip Kemble the actor. Within nine days they had resolved to issue one hundred shares at £500 each to assist the rebuilding and had selected their architect. This was Robert Smirke, the son of a well-known painter and illustrator of the same name. Smirke junior, then not quite twenty-eight, was already acquiring a reputation

13 Sir Robert Smirke, R.A. (1780-1867) architect of the second Theatre Royal, Covent Garden

6 *The Morning Chronicle* 24 September 1782
7 *The World*, 15 September 1792

14 Playbill for the opening night of the second Theatre Royal, Covent Garden, 18 September 1809

The Publick are respectfully informed that the

New Theatre Royal, Covent-Garden,
WILL BE OPENED
This present MONDAY, Sept. 18, 1809,
With the Tragedy of

MACBETH.

With entirely new Scenery, Dresses, & Decorations.
The Overture and Symphonies between the Acts by Mr. WARE.
The Vocal Music by MATTHEW LOCK.
Duncan, King of Scotland, by Mr. CHAPMAN,
Malcolm by Mr. CLAREMONT,   Donalbain by Mr. MENAGE,
Macbeth by Mr. KEMBLE,   Macduff by Mr. C. KEMBLE,
Banquo by Mr. MURRAY,   Fleance by M. BRISTOW,
Lenox by Mr. CRESWELL,   Rosse by Mr. BRINTON,
Siward Mr ATKINS, Seyton Mr JEFFERIES, Physician Mr DAVENPORT
Officers, Mess. Thompson & Wilde,   Chamberlains, Mess. Heath & Truman
Gentlemen, Mess. Brown, Grant, Holland. Louis. Powers, Sarjant,
Lady Macbeth by Mrs. SIDDONS.
Gentlewoman by Mrs HUMPHRIES,
Ladies Mesdames Bologna, L Bologna, Cox, Cranfield Follett, Whitmore,
Apparitions, Mr. Field, Miss S. Goodwin, Miss C. Goodwin,
Hecat' by Mr BELLAMY, Witches, Mess. BLANCHARD, FARLEY, SIMMONS

To which will be added the musical Entertainment of

The QUAKER.

Steady by Mr. INCLEDON,   Easy by Mr. DAVENPORT,
Lubin by Mr. TAYLOR,   Solomon by Mr. LISTON,
John by Mr HOLLAND,   Thomas by Mr. TRUMAN,
Gillian Miss BOLTON, Cecily Miss LESERVE, Floretta Mrs LISTON.
Before the Play, an Occasional Address on the opening of the Theatre,
Will be spoken by Mr. KEMBLE.
Places for the Boxes to be taken of Mr. Brandon, at the Box Office in Hart-Street
The Doors will be opened at HALF past FIVE, and the Play begin at HALF past SIX.

THE PROPRIETORS, having completed the NEW THEATRE within the time originally promised, beg leave respectfully to state to the Publick the absolute necessity that compels them to make the following advance on the prices of admission:
FIRST PRICE.   HALF PRICE.
BOXES, Seven Shillings.   Three Shillings and Sixpence.
PIT,   Four Shillings,   Two Shillings, as usual.
The LOWER and UPPER GALLERIES will remain at the old Prices.
On the late calamitous destruction of their property, the Proprietors, encouraged by the remembrance of former patronage, instantly and cheerfully applied themselves to the erection of a new Theatre, judging it impolitic that, without enlarging the audience-part of the edifice, it might be afforded materially improved accommodation and security, and at the same time present an additional ornament to the Metropolis of the British Empire This, their most anxious wish, they flatter themselves, they have solidly effected, not only within the short space of ten months from the laying of the foundations, but under the enormously expensive disadvantage of circumstances singularly unfavourable to building—When it is known that no less a sum than one hundred and fifty thousand pounds has been expended in order to render this Theatre worthy of British Spectators, and of the Genius of their native Poets:—when, in this undertaking, the inevitable accumulation of, at least, a sixfold rentage is positively stated to be incurred;—and when, in addition to these pressing incumbrances, the encreasing and rapidly encreasing prices of every article indispensable to dramatick representations come to be considered—the Proprietors persuade themselves that in their proposed regulation they shall be honoured with the concurrence of an enlightened & liberal Publick.

The attention of the Publick is requested to the following description of the
Entrances to the new Theatre.

BOXES.
The principal Entrance is at the Portico in Bow-street, leading to the stone Hall and Staircase.
The West Entrance is in Prince's-Place, leading from the Piazza in Covent-Garden to the stone Staircase and Ante-room.

PIT.
The principal Entrance is from the Piazza, through Bedford-Avenue, leading by five doors to the stone Vestibule and Staircases.
The East Entrance is in the Arcade, South of the Portico in Bow-Street, leading to the same Vestibule and Staircases.

LOWER GALLERY.
The principal Entrance is from the Piazza, through Bedford-Avenue.

LOWER and UPPER GALLERIES.
The Entrance is at the Eastern extremity of Bedford-Avenue in Bow-Street.

ANNUAL BOXES.
The Entrances are in Prince's-Place, leading from Hart-Street;—and in the Arcade, North of the Portico in Bow-Street.

Ladies and Gentlemen going to the Theatre by any of the Entrances in Bow-Street, are requested to order their Coachmen to set down with their horses heads towards Long-Acre,—and to drive off through Little Bow-Street.
Ladies and Gentlemen coming to the Annual Boxes in Prince's-Place, are requested to order their Coachmen to drive to the Theatre through Long-Acre and down James-Street into Hart-Street,—or through Covent-Garden up James-Street into Hart-Street,—and to drive from the Theatre through the same Streets.

as a reliable, meticulous architect and as an enthusiast for the newly fashionable Greek Revival. At Covent Garden he gave his employers something thoroughly well built, yet also novel and startling: London's first major building in the Greek Doric manner, and the modern world's first 'Grecian' theatre. Of the three Covent Garden theatres, without doubt Smirke's is the one that stands out for impressiveness and originality. Work began late in 1808, and the theatre re-opened with *Macbeth* on 18 September 1809.

Smirke's theatre followed the alignment of the previous building, with the stage and workrooms at the north end, the auditorium at the south end, and the main entrance towards Bow Street. But unlike the first theatre this was a freestanding building, affording plenty of space for display. Smirke seized his opportunity with a young man's enthusiasm. Towards Bow Street he placed a ponderous, symmetrical front of stone and stucco with a few widely spaced openings on the ground floor leading into a cavernous arcade, corresponding windows above and, in the centre, a solemn Greek portico resting on four hefty Doric columns. All this was based on the Parthenon, which Smirke had visited a few years before. At the ends of the front, niches contained statues in artificial stone by John Flaxman (the Comic Muse) and J.C. Rossi (the Tragic Muse); also by Flaxman and Rossi were two long friezes which ran high up along the front on either side of the portico. (The statues and friezes were salvaged after the fire of 1856, and in altered format still adorn the front of the present Opera House.) Behind this great frontispiece, the bulk of the main theatre loomed up dramatically. To give this part of the building extra severity, Smirke hid its conventionally pitched roof behind a screen wall, which he then breached six times in line with the openings of the front below, letting the eaves protrude in a sombre manner.

Inside the theatre, what especially struck early observers was the stately route traversed by patrons who used the Bow Street entrance on the way to their boxes. Then as now, they entered the foyer and turned left up the principal staircase. It is no disparagement to the present approaches to admit that Smirke's sequence was far nobler: up a single great flight beneath a vault sustained on black Ionic columns, straight on into an ante-room centred upon a larger-than-life effigy of Shakespeare by Rossi, right into a curving lobby behind the auditorium, and so to one's seat; or, if time allowed, into one of two handsome, lengthy, Hellenic saloons, where refreshments were served amidst edifying 'casts from the antique'.

Plate 1 The auditorium of Edward Shepherd's theatre shortly before the fire of 1808, showing Handel's organ on the stage

Plate 2 The auditorium of Sir Robert Smirke's theatre in 1810

Plate 3 The Theatre
Royal, Covent Garden in
1810

Plate 4 The vast Gothic
Hall created by Messrs
Grieve for the Free
Trade Bazaar, May 1845

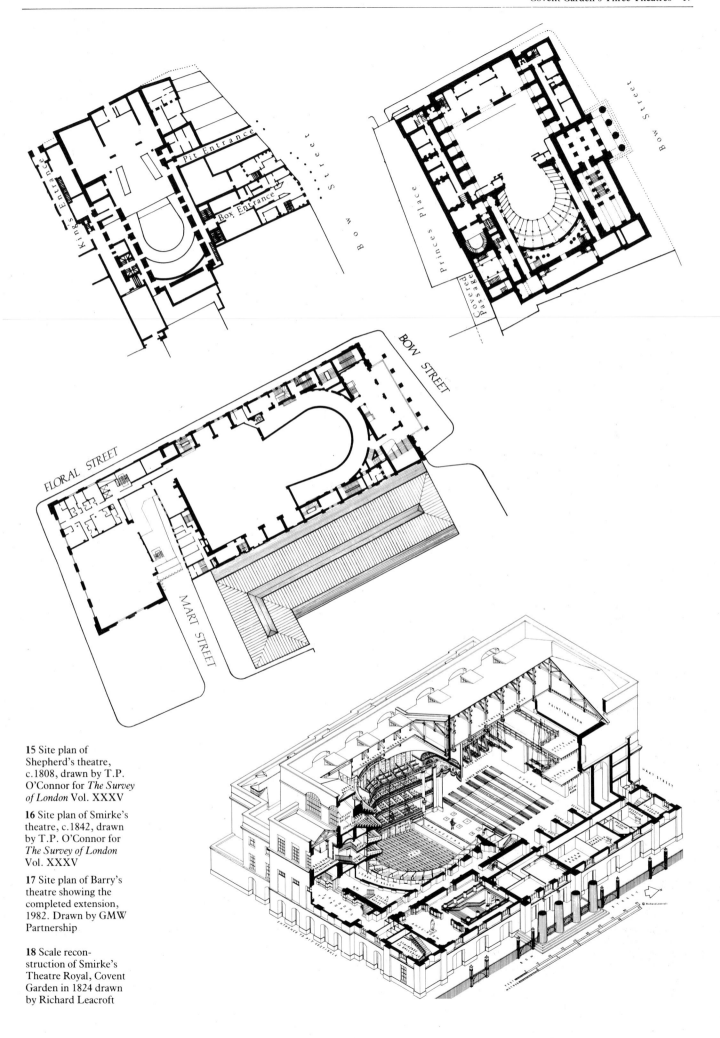

15 Site plan of Shepherd's theatre, c.1808, drawn by T.P. O'Connor for *The Survey of London* Vol. XXXV

16 Site plan of Smirke's theatre, c.1842, drawn by T.P. O'Connor for *The Survey of London* Vol. XXXV

17 Site plan of Barry's theatre showing the completed extension, 1982. Drawn by GMW Partnership

18 Scale reconstruction of Smirke's Theatre Royal, Covent Garden in 1824 drawn by Richard Leacroft

19 Plan of Smirke's theatre drawn at first-tier level, 1824

20 Foundation stone of the second theatre now located in the Gentlemen Chorus washroom

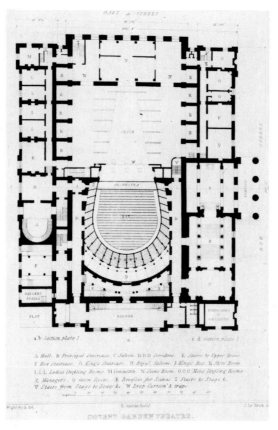

21 Saloon to the Private Boxes, 1810

22 The Grand Staircase at Covent Garden Theatre on the evening of a *bal masqué*, 1844

The theatre itself was surprisingly orthodox and seems to have owed a great deal to Holland's Drury Lane. Here again were the horseshoe tiers (mostly divided into boxes), the thin cast-iron columns, the apron in front of a deep proscenium arch and the raked-back stage behind. One novel feature was short-lived: a series of arches popularly known as the 'pigeon holes', squeezed in just below the ceiling to accommodate the 'one-shilling gallery'. Above these, the ceiling was gently dished. Most of the surface ornament was of plaster, supplied by Francis Bernasconi. The original colour scheme of the boxes was a Grecian pink, set off by mahogany woodwork, but by 1825 (when various structural changes had been made) this had given way to a more conventional 'subdued yellow, relieved by white, and superbly enriched with gilding'.[8] The detailing of the interior was generally admired; Weber, for instance, characterized it as 'a beautifully decorated, but not overwhelmingly large house'.[9]

When Smirke's theatre was erected, new methods of construction and servicing were just starting to be developed for specialized buildings of this kind. The main contractor for the theatre, Alexander Copland, was famed for combining speed with solid construction, having gained his reputation by building barracks at the height of the Napoleonic invasion scare a few years before. So far as is known the structure was straightforward and the roof was of wood not iron, but the walls were certainly reinforced with great baulks of timber at regular intervals, and a good deal of hidden iron was used in addition to the slender columns that supported the galleries.

As for the services, Smirke's building appears to have been the first centrally heated theatre in Britain. A system of steam-heating and ventilation was supplied by the great Birmingham firm of Boulton and Watt, who had pioneered the technique for mills, employing the Watt steam engine. This was supplemented in 1817 by an eccentric French émigré, half genius and half charlatan, the Marquis de Chabannes, whose stoves (or *calorifères fumivores*) long adorned the entrances and stairway. Meanwhile in 1815 gas lighting arrived, first tentatively installed in the public rooms and approaches and then in 1817 transferred to the auditorium, where a splendid gas chandelier was hung from the centre. Playgoers were besotted with this

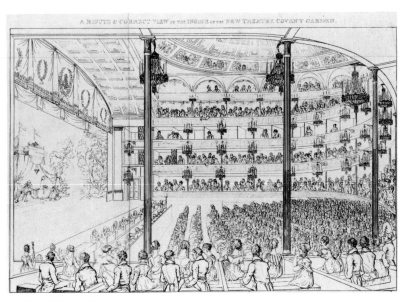

23 The auditorium in 1810

24 The auditorium in 1815, drawing by J. Gleadah

8 J. Britton and A. Pugin, *Illustrations of the Public Buildings of London*, vol 1, 1825, p 220
9 John Warrack, *Carl Maria von Weber*, 1968, p 333

innovation, and a contemporary guidebook commented: 'the galleries appear to be screened from the glare which pours down in a flood of harmless lustre on the stage, the boxes, and the pit.'[10] Gas of course presaged a revolution in theatrical presentation, but it also brought dangers and inconveniences. Covent Garden experimented for a time with making its own oil gas, which produced a pretty but notoriously volatile light, before settling down to coal gas from the mains. In addition, the great chandelier had to be lit by the perilous method of a gasman with a long waxed staff leaning out from the vent hole in the dome over the centre of the auditorium. Good ventilation was vital, because of the stifling discomfort which attended the use of unpurified gas in its early days; in 1828 the management had to issue a notice apologising for inconveniences suffered from gaslight, and promising to reinstate some of the old oil lamps.

25 Playbill announcing the closure of the theatre for the removal of gas appliances, 1828

Covent-Garden Theatre.

Closed for One Week

ADDRESS.

WHEN the brilliancy of GAS illumination attracted Public admiration, the Proprietors of this Theatre anxious to adopt every Improvement which would give brilliancy to the Scenery, and the appearance of the Theatre, introduced it; and to prevent the accidents which the best Street illumination is liable to, they at a great expense constructed Gasometers: finding however that with the utmost care and skill, the introduction of Gas in the audience part of the Theatre, produced an offensive odour, and the Public having suffered inconvenience and disappointment in their amusements, by the mischievous agency of some malignant and interested Persons; the Proprietors have determined to remove the Gas, not only from the Box Circles, but from all internal avenues leading to them, as well as to the Pit and Galleries.

But as this important Alteration cannot be effectually done, while the Theatre is nightly open, without the Public being put to inconvenience, the Managers have determined to submit to the heavy loss of Closing their Theatre, rather than allow the Public to suffer any drawback to their Theatrical Enjoyments.

The Public is in consequence respectfully informed, that as the proposed Improvements cannot be executed in less than a Week, the Theatre will remain

CLOSED TILL MONDAY,

THE 24th INSTANT;

when they hope to welcome the Public to a Theatre, where no Expense will be spared, or Zeal remitted, to render it worthy the liberal Patronage it has ever enjoyed.

J. FAWCETT, Stage Manager.

Printed by W. Reynell, Little Pulteney Street.

10 *Leigh's New Picture of London*, 1819, pp 434-6
11 *The Builder*, 6 October 1855

Smirke's theatre turned out to be punitively costly to its promoters. The old Covent Garden theatre had been underinsured, and if Harris and Kemble expected to cover the expense of rebuilding out of the £45,000 they extracted from the insurers plus the £50,000 they raised in shares, they were sadly deceived. The new building cost a staggering £187,888, more than twice as much as Holland's Drury Lane and over £36,000 more than the theatre built by Benjamin Wyatt to succeed it in 1811-12, which could hold about 3,100 as against Covent Garden's normal figure of about 2,800. The extravagant rebuilding of both 'Patent' theatres helps to explain the slow decline in their fortunes over the ensuing thirty years. Trouble began right from the start at Covent Garden, with the 'OP' or Old Price riots. Protests often broke out when a theatre was altered and re-opened with higher prices or fewer cheap seats to recoup costs. But the 'OP riots' of 1809 were so unusually prolonged and bitter that Harris and Kemble had no option but to give way. A particular complaint was that space for ordinary patrons had been reduced in favour of private shareholders, who enjoyed private boxes with ante-rooms: 'it got bruited about that the object was to admit of assignations,' alleged a Victorian critic, 'so that, at length, no respectable lady could appear in these boxes.'[11]

Nevertheless, under first John Philip Kemble and then his brother Charles, Covent Garden kept up a high dramatic reputation for twenty years after the re-opening. The grand tone of Smirke's theatre, with its painted Doric backdrop representing a 'Temple of British Drama', suited the company's specialities at this period – Shakespeare, tragedy and romantic opera. The 1820s were perhaps the heyday of scene-painting at Covent Garden. By now the old formality of the eighteenth-century wings and backdrop settings was disappearing, and John Henderson Grieve and his two sons became celebrated for devising a plethora of romantic and picturesque effects in their stead, notably for popular stage versions of Sir Walter Scott's novels. Pugin, the great Gothic revivalist, was briefly embroiled at Covent Garden with the Grieves as a stage-struck young man in the 1820s.

The proprietors were losing money for much of this period. So in 1832, the year of Covent Garden's centenary, they began leasing the theatre out for restricted periods, for instance to the great W.C.Macready and to the comedian C.J.Mathews and his wife Madame Vestris. Yet by 1843, when the monopoly of the 'Patent theatres' was finally abolished, Covent Garden was in low water and was as much in demand for meetings as for plays or concerts.

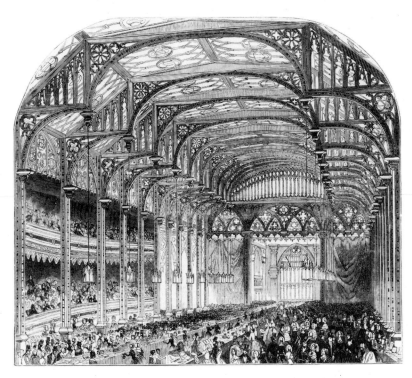

26 The theatre decorated
for the Anti-Corn Law
League's Free Trade
Bazaar in May 1845

27 Work in progress on
the reconstruction of the
interior, December 1846

A new lease of life came in 1847, the year in which opera established itself as the central activity of Covent Garden. Discontent had long been brewing at the Queen's Theatre, Haymarket, hitherto the regular venue for Italian opera. Now a band of rebels backed by Cramer, Beale and Company, music publishers, and led by the conductor Michael Costa and by Giuseppe Persiani, whose wife was one of the main draws at the Haymarket, seceded and took over Covent Garden. As usual, alterations and embellishments had to be made to accommodate the 'Royal Italian Opera Company', and who better to carry them out than Italians? Accordingly, Benedetto (or Benedict) Albano came in at the instigation of his fellow-Neapolitan, Costa, to direct operations. Albano was a truly operatic figure, a cloak-and-dagger radical who had sought refuge in Britain in the 1820s after being implicated in the assassination of the police chief of Naples, and who later practised as an architect and engineer in France. At Covent Garden, Albano in 1846-7 remodelled the approaches, put in new fire-resisting staircases and gutted the auditorium so as to enlarge the pit and the orchestra and form no less than six tiers, set back to a new line. The apron stage was reduced almost to nothing and the proscenium widened to forty-six feet. The

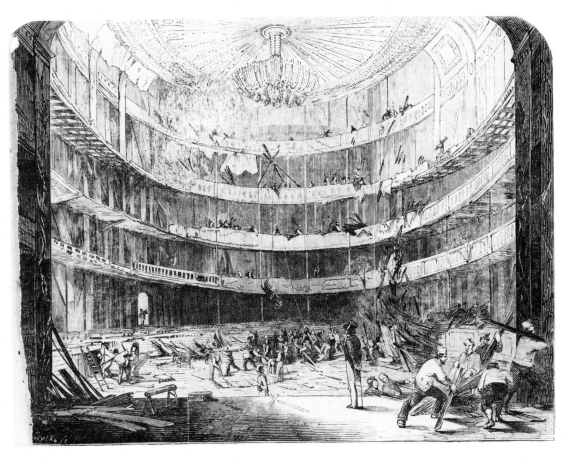

28 Poster for a Concert organised by J.H. Anderson, the self-styled 'Wizard of the North'. It was after one of his *bal masqués* that the second Theatre Royal, Covent Garden was destroyed by fire

29 Interior of the Royal Italian Opera House, opened on 6 April 1847

ceiling was decorated by Domenico Ferri, an Italian known for his theatrical work in Paris, with help from Signor Verardi, Monsieur Zarra and a lone Englishman, Ponsonby, who worked in a hemp-based type of plaster patented by Albano.

As fully Italian a theatre as ever existed in England, the building opened once again with Rossini's *Semiramide* on 6 April 1847. But the first season of the Royal Italian Opera House proved financially disastrous. At this point Frederick Gye, son of the proprietor of Vauxhall Gardens, came to the rescue. Gye was to lead Covent Garden out of the wilderness towards the promised land of operatic prosperity. In this he was at first aided by Albano's reconstruction, which was agreed to be a success and probably influenced the planning of the present building.

But first another conflagration had to be endured. In 1855-6 Gye sublet Covent Garden to the self-styled 'artist in natural magic' and 'Wizard of the North', J.H. Anderson, an impresario of conjuring, pantomime and other motley entertainments. In the early hours of 5 March 1856 a *bal masqué* at the end of a 'Grand Complimentary Benefit and Dramatic Gala' was drawing to a close. The band was just striking

30 Destruction by fire of the second Theatre Royal, Covent Garden, 5 March 1856

31 Photograph of the ruins, March 1856

up 'God Save the Queen' when the ceiling was found to be on fire, the blaze having started in the carpenters' workshop over the stage. By six o'clock the building was doomed, for during his reconstruction, Albano had unwisely removed the wall inserted by Smirke over the proscenium arch between the stage and the auditorium, so that the fire was able to spread without hindrance throughout the building. Gye was going to have to start all over again.

SUPPLEMENT TO THE

THE ROYAL ITAL

THE CRUSH ROOM.

THE AUDITORIUM.

32 Views of the Royal
Italian Opera House and
Floral Hall, 1882

SPORTING AND DRAMATIC NEWS.—April 15, 1882.

OPERA HOUSE, COVENT GARDEN.

EXTERIOR.   INTERIOR OF FLORAL HALL.

33 Her Majesty Queen Victoria arriving to inspect the ruins of Smirke's theatre, 14 March 1856

The Present Theatre and
The Floral Hall

34 Frederick Gye (1809-78), Manager of the Royal Italian Opera, Covent Garden 1849-77

After the fire of 1856, it was far from certain that Covent Garden Theatre would continue. Rumours flew the rounds: perhaps the market would be extended, or St Paul's Church would be moved to the site, or even the Law Courts. All this was to reckon without Frederick Gye's indomitability. Though he had lost some £30,000, he immediately hired the Lyceum for the summer opera season in 1856. Meanwhile with the support of his landlord the Duke of Bedford, he resolved upon returning to the old site.

When Gye's rebuilding scheme matured, it turned out to be powerfully imbued with his somewhat headstrong personality. In 1842, nine years before the Crystal Palace had revealed the potential of prefabricated architecture, Gye had conceived of a 'gigantic arcade' of iron and glass stretching all the way from Bank to Trafalgar Square; this was to include 'an extensive flower market' - a feature perhaps borrowed from the Marché aux Fleurs in Paris. Gye now revived this idea by deciding to place a 'Floral Hall' alongside a new Covent Garden concert hall or theatre. By leasing extra ground he was able to fit both buildings on to the site, with the theatre running from east to west instead of north to

south, as formerly. The Floral Hall, Gye no doubt hoped, would help to provide the extra space needed for the Covent Garden Market and might also subsidise the theatre.

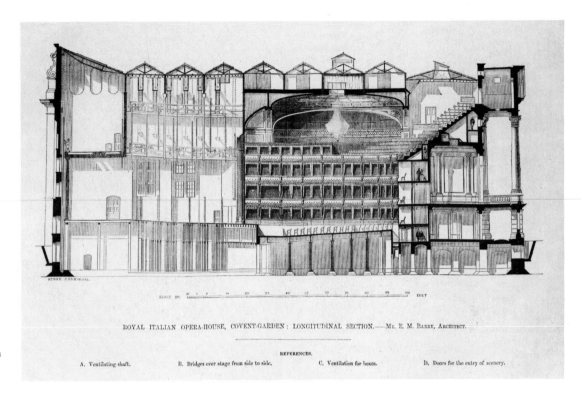

ROYAL ITALIAN OPERA-HOUSE, COVENT-GARDEN: LONGITUDINAL SECTION.—Mr. E. M. BARRY, ARCHITECT.

REFERENCES.

A. Ventilating shaft.   B. Bridges over stage from side to side.   C. Ventilation for boxes.   D. Doors for the entry of scenery.

35 Longitudinal section of the Royal Italian Opera House

36 E.M. Barry, R.A. (1830-80) architect of the present theatre

To carry out the project Gye possibly first approached Fox and Henderson, the chief contractors for the Crystal Palace, and Sir Charles Barry, whose interest he had courted over his arcade scheme of 1842. But Barry was close to retirement, so the designing of the new theatre fell instead to his son Edward Middleton Barry, who as yet had built little of his own. For a second time, therefore, the perilous task of raising a new theatre at Covent Garden was entrusted to a young man of limited experience. Luckily E.M.Barry was as level-headed as Smirke, and lacked Smirke's obsession with costly Greek formality; the mixed French and Italian classicism by now traditional to theatres suited him well. So in point of style, the third Covent Garden Theatre was not destined to be original, merely dignified and appropriate.

In fact Barry was just one of several partners of equal stature who, besides working on Gye's great enterprise, also advanced money towards it, and so had strong interests in hastening it to success. The builders appointed, Charles and Thomas Lucas of Lowestoft, were young, energetic and ambitious men who were well used to fulfilling complex public works contracts at speed; they underwrote the project to the tune of more than £20,000. Another important mortgagee was Henry Grissell, whose firm made and fixed all the iron for the Royal Opera House and the Floral Hall. Like the Lucases, Grissell had prospered from the rash of railways, docks and other great engineering

labours of the 1840s and '50s. He also supplied ironwork for the Houses of Parliament and specialized in the manufacture of prefabricated iron buildings. Since both the Floral Hall and the theatre depended upon up-to-date techniques of iron construction, Grissell's role as engineer was crucial.

Others assisted Gye in the fitting-up and decoration of the theatre. For the technical arrangement of the stage he turned to William

37 The Flaxman-Rossi frieze that survived the fire of 1856 and is incorporated in the façade of the present theatre

Roxby Beverley, the most original and mechanically inclined 'scenic artist' of the day. And in the finishing of the auditorium, Barry was regretfully obliged to play second fiddle to Raffaelle Monti, an Italian sculptor and Risorgimento exile keen to make a name in England in the field of decorative arts.

The designs were ready in March 1857. For the time being the Floral Hall was delayed and only the Opera House went ahead. Work commenced in September and was prosecuted with the ruthless haste peculiar to theatre-building; the fabric rose 'with Aladdin-like celerity out of the ashes of its predecessor'.[12] The Lucases used every means they could to speed the work on. During the winter the men were kitted out with black waterproof suits against the weather. In the last weeks there were 1,200 men on site and several fatal accidents occurred; very close to the end, the chief mason himself stepped back to admire a portion of completed work, tumbled down and was killed. Most of the joinery, including the whole framework of the auditorium ceiling, was prefabricated in Lucas Brothers' Lowestoft works and then reassembled in the building. Eventually, with the scaffolding barely off the portico and Gye away recuperating from a nervous collapse, the theatre opened with *Les Huguenots* on Saturday, 15 May 1858. The audience took so long to reach their seats from Barry's confined and unfamiliar approaches and the performance was so drawn out, that Sunday had crept in by the time that the penultimate act reached its close. Out of respect for the Sabbath the management announced the omission of the last act, to public disgust.

Despite this débâcle, the new theatre soon proved itself practical, adaptable and serviceable. Allegedly it cost £80,000, or less than half the £180,000 lavished on the second Covent Garden theatre. Certainly it occupied less ground than its predecessor. Yet it made up

for this with greater height and could accommodate almost as many people as before, that is to say nearly 2,000 for opera and 3,000 for other performances and functions.

Externally, Barry's opera house is characteristic of the classicism current throughout nineteenth-century Europe for public buildings. The one oddity about the elevations, considering their date, is that they are all stuccoed. At first, Frederick Gye seems for economy's sake to have proposed side elevations of brick and a stucco front without a portico. But the Bedford Estate insisted on retaining some of the previous theatre's dignity, so Gye was grudgingly obliged to build the portico and plaster the sides of the building. In other ways too the present theatre carries over features from its predecessor. On the main Bow Street front, Barry arranged his great Corinthian frontispiece around the statues and reliefs by Flaxman and Rossi, practically the only items to be salvaged from the Smirke theatre. Originally these were to be supplemented with new sculpture for the tympanum, apex and corners of the pediment, but economies put paid to that. So the haphazardly re-ordered Flaxman and Rossi figures now provide the only substantial ornament on the Bow Street front. Their interest would be enhanced if the original dark blue ground behind the reliefs could be restored. The main front is more severely marred today by the cluttered appearance of the portico; both the crush bar, jammed in behind the columns in 1899, and the infill which in 1950-1 replaced the covered carriageway, detract from the proportions of Barry's architecture.

Inside the theatre, the public spaces betray the constraints under which Gye and Barry laboured. By European standards they are

12 *The Building News*, 14 May 1858

extraordinarily restricted. Barry's foyer and grand staircase loosely follow the plan of the old Smirke theatre. Originally, patrons emerged from their carriages directly into a long, low hall paved with encaustic tiles; they then turned left up the stairs to attain greater height and elegance above. Today, the foyer's appearance dates mainly from the enlargement and redecoration of 1950-1. Busts of Patti and Melba flank the main entrance to the stalls, while off to the right the statue of Frederick Gye stands close to the position of his original private office.

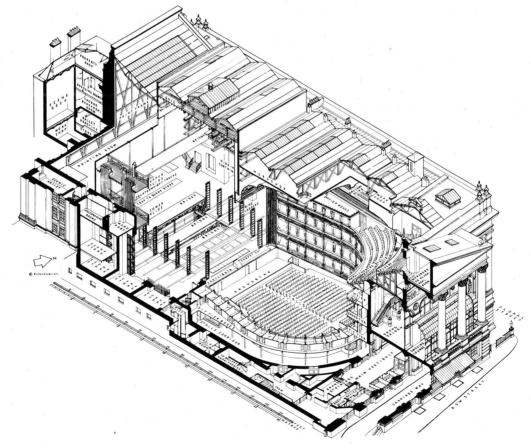

38 Scale reconstruction of the Royal Opera House including E.O. Sachs' alterations of 1899-1901, drawn by Richard Leacroft

39 The auditorium in 1858 during a performance of Verdi's *Il trovatore*

40 The foyer in 1937

41 The Grand Staircase in 1948

By contrast, the grand staircase has altered little; its slow and dignified ascent compensates for parsimony elsewhere. At its head is the crush room, a handsome pilastered saloon as tall as it is wide. As planned by Barry it was eighty feet long, lit by gas chandeliers, and terminated with two free-standing columns, a fireplace and a buffet. Later, the north end of the room was cut off, and a double staircase placed along the side wall to allow access to balcony level. Because of overcrowding, the connecting 'conservatory-bar' was substituted for the original open terrace over the portico in 1899. The large paintings in this room and at the top of the main stair are all by the seventeenth-century Dutch artist Augustyn Terwesten; they too appear to have been installed in 1899.

Like most freestanding Victorian theatres, Covent Garden consists of an open void for the auditorium and stage, flanked at the sides by a string of staircases, corridors and rooms. In order to span the void, Barry and his engineer Grissell thickened up the flanking walls, external and internal, and turned them into supports for the ends of eight huge wrought-iron lattice girders, 96 feet long, 9 feet high and

21 feet apart, which span the width of the auditorium and stage. The ceiling of the auditorium and much of the stage machinery was hung from these girders. Each was calculated to support 150 tons, and two were tested in Grissell's works to a tolerance of 300 tons. The main roof above them is subdivided into small pitched roofs running from girder to girder and is invisible from close to.

Within this mighty framework, the auditorium stands quite independently. Barry wrote of it: 'the boxes and corridors are, in fact, a separate structure of iron, stone and wood, erected inside the chamber formed by the main walls of the building'.[13] The tiers of boxes are cantilevered out on hidden iron girders so that columns do not encroach on the fronts of the boxes and interfere with the sight lines.

Despite these rigid structures, the auditorium was meant to be flexible. Like the Smirke theatre in its later days, E.M.Barry's building at first functioned as an opera house for only a short summer season; for the rest of the year it was leased out for pantomines, concerts, balls and meetings. So the proscenium could be adjusted in width, the floor of the stalls could be raised and levelled out at the height of the stage or the first tier of boxes, and the partitions between the boxes could be removed.

It seems likely that Barry's arrangement of the auditorium derived, on Gye's instructions, from the Smirke theatre as reconstructed by Benedetto Albano, which had been admired equally for its acoustics and its appearance. The ground floor was divided into eleven rows of pit stalls in front and a restricted pit behind. Above this were four horseshoe tiers (two less than in Albano's theatre), from the highest of which a

deep amphitheatre and gallery were raked sharply back. There were boxes, originally 121 in number, all around the three main tiers and even at the sides of the amphitheatre. Except at the sides of the grand and balcony tiers, these have disappeared today. Among the survivors are the double-width Royal Box on the north side of the grand tier and, next to it, the Bedford Box (wrung out of the hard-pressed Gye as part of the original building agreement); both these have their own connecting private room, access and street entrance from Floral Street. The royal suite shows signs of a redecoration to the fancy of Edward VII, and includes a cosy, cabin-like smoking room.

Unquestionably the handsomest feature of the auditorium is the low saucer ceiling, with its deep, elliptical arches at the sides. The ceiling appears to be supported on massive piers, but in reality the whole structure hangs from the girders above. It was mostly designed by E.M.Barry and was executed by George Jackson and Sons in a mixture of papier-mâché and fibrous plaster. In shape the ceiling owes much to the saucer domes used a generation earlier by Soane, but its detailing reflects the taste of C.R.Cockerell's interiors at St George's Hall, Liverpool. The gilded proscenium arch with its twisted columns was also designed by Barry and carried out by Jacksons. Elsewhere in the decoration of the auditorium, Barry was passed over by Gye in favour of Raffaelle Monti, the Italian sculptor and designer. Monti's box fronts follow a swelling, rococo line of which Barry explicitly disapproved; they are ornamented with elegant winged nymphs who increase in maturity from tier to tier. Also Monti's is the relief over the proscenium arch, in the manner

42 The King's Smoking Room in 1948

43 The carriage way in 1937

13 *R.I.B.A. Transactions*, vol 10, 1859-60, pp 53-64

of the Portland vase; it depicts allegories of Music and Poetry separated by the bust of Queen Victoria, who determinedly sets her face towards the latter.

The present colours of the auditorium match the original scheme. Gold, crimson and ivory are of course traditional to the theatre, while the arresting 'cerulean blue' of the saucer dome follows an old custom of painting playhouse ceilings a sky colour in deference to the open-air theatres of antiquity. The original ensemble would have been enhanced by the generous rose-coloured hangings provided for all the boxes. The first drop-curtain was also presumably red. Later, the dominant colour of the auditorium was changed to green; red returned to favour in 1911, and with it came a new pair of hydraulically operated drop-curtains in red and gold, embroidered with the royal monogram – a practice still continued.

44 The auditorium in 1948

Originally the auditorium was lit by a great central chandelier supplied by Jonas Defries and Son, gas engineers. The pierced aperture in the centre of the ceiling above served to carry off its fumes, and also to raise and lower the chandelier for the purposes of lighting and cleaning. To supplement this central lustre, the tier fronts were provided with gas brackets. Until the 1890s, the lights were merely dimmed during performances, but they were then extinguished following the practice at Bayreuth. This innovation was resisted by the old habitués, 'who objected to sitting through *Der Ring des Nibelungen* in a darkened auditorium which demanded and focussed their attention on the stage'.[14] The extinguishing of lights was made possible by the advent of electricity. The brackets on the tier fronts were converted first, but the great chandelier did not disappear until 1899-1900, when the present pretty individual pendant lights were installed in the ceiling.

The stage was laid out by Barry according to the directions of the scene painter William Beverley in association with Gye's master carpenter and 'machinist', Henry Sloman. It had a modest apron front, 'from which the principal artistes commonly sing'.[15] The stage proper was raked to a depth of sixty feet, was ninety feet wide and incorporated five traps; the sides and back were fixed, but most of the centre could be removed for the purpose of raising sets. There were no wings of the old-fashioned type, as most of the scenery hung above or below the stage; at the sides were scene docks for storage, and a recess for an organ. The only survivals from the Barry stage today are the wooden fly galleries, raked to accord with the level of the original floor, and the generous top-lit painting room, situated above the back stage and equipped with a paint frame from which completed backcloths are lowered on to the stage below. Otherwise the present stage dates almost entirely from 1900-01.

14 Terence Rees, *Theatre Lighting in the Age of Gas*, 1978, p 188
15 *The Builder*, 18 February 1860

Plate 5 An early print of the exterior of the present theatre, designed by E.M. Barry

Royal Italian Opera, Covent Garden

Plate 6 The auditorium during an orchestral rehearsal, 1982

Plate 7 The Floral Hall decorated for a ball in the late nineteenth century

45 The auditorium
*c.*1950, showing the
fleur-de-lys pattern on
the upholstery

With the Opera House completed, Gye and his team (E.M.Barry, Henry Grissell and the Lucas Brothers) proceeded with the Floral Hall. Here, well before work began in April 1858, difficulties began to dog the whole enterprise. Gye's first thought was to erect a cheap building functioning frankly as a market, with a pitched roof of iron and glass but no columns and no frontage to the Piazza. The Bedford Estate disliked this idea; so a compromise was reached, involving a more ornamental and costly design in the style of a conservatory. This was to be a 'show' attraction rivalling the theatre – a mini-Crystal Palace on an L-shaped plan with a round-arched roof, a high glass dome at the intersection of the arms, and two pretty fan-like facades, one towards Bow Street and the other facing the Piazza. It was to be a fashionable market by day, selling 'flowers of a more expensive kind for which a much increased demand has arisen'[16], and a concert hall by night.

Once the Floral Hall had been completed, the dispute broke out openly. The Bedford Estate refused to take space in the building and opened their own flower market in existing premises nearby; here in due course a special building (now the London Transport Museum) was built in 1871-2. Gye was left with a white elephant which never paid its way. At first he put on a brave face and the Floral Hall opened in March 1860, gaily decked out for a 'Grand Volunteers' Ball'. For a time concerts were held with the orchestra under the dome, but the very type of

construction which made the building suitable for market trading also rendered it acoustically hopeless. Meanwhile the Bedford Estate made intermittent objections to Gye's policies and the lettings fell off. Gye published a pamphlet complaining bitterly of unfair treatment, but it was to no avail: the Floral Hall was a flop. In 1887, the Bedford Estate bought it back and ignominiously converted it into a 'foreign fruit market'. Even this was not the final humiliation: in 1956 a fire destroyed the dome and roof. The latter alone was replaced, and in a simplified form which deprived this hitherto beautiful building of nearly all its interest. Today it stands forlorn, stacked with scenery and props from the Opera House and awaiting a decision upon its fate.

The fiasco of the Floral Hall cast a shadow over the latter years of Frederick Gye. Until his sudden death in a shooting accident in 1878, he continued to run Covent Garden with as much acumen as before, but the caution of his programming reflected the sums still owing on the two buildings. His son Ernest Gye succeeded him, but gave up the business in 1883-4. There ensued sixteen years of varying managements, of which those musically best remembered were the seasons of opera presented by Sir Augustus Harris from 1888 until 1896.

16 Bedford Office, annual report for 1856

46 Cleaning the dome of the Floral Hall, between the wars

47 The fire that destroyed the Floral Hall dome in 1956

As money was short during most of this period, the theatre underwent few alterations. One important change was made to improve the audience's safety after Captain Shaw, the redoubtable commander of the Metropolitan Fire Brigade, investigated all the main London theatres in 1882. To prevent a fire from spreading from the stage to the auditorium or vice versa, as had happened in 1856, a wall was carried up over the proscenium to a point above the roof, the arch itself acquired its first safety curtain, and the various openings between the front and back of the house were fitted with iron doors.

Safety was further improved with the advent of electricity, first installed at Covent Garden in 1883. It did not entirely replace gas lighting until 1899-1901, when important alterations occurred. In 1899 the 'Grand Opera Syndicate Limited', consisting chiefly of Sir Augustus Harris's old backers, took over with a view to revitalizing Covent Garden. The first changes made were in the front of the house, notably the insertion of the present bar over the entrance, next to the crush room. But this scarcely helped to improve the standards of production. These were the days of Wagnerian opera, requiring effects far grander than the clever tricks with traps and 'transformations' for which Beverley and Barry had equipped their stage; the Covent Garden stage was acknowledged to be 'woefully behind the times' and especially primitive compared to what was available in German opera houses.[17]

17 *The Sketch*, 24 April 1901

So the Syndicate brought in the one person in England ideally qualified to solve the problem, a young half-German architect called Edwin O. Sachs. Sachs had three passions in life – architecture, the theatre and fires. He had studied architecture in Berlin and spent a whole year as a 'ranker' with the fire brigade there. Moving to London, he compiled a great treatise on modern opera houses and theatres and founded the British Fire Prevention Committee. The Covent Garden commission, carried out in 1900-01, followed Sachs's electrification of the Drury Lane stage on the latest German principles in 1898. He gutted the entire stage, leaving only Barry's fly galleries. The whole area was deepened and heightened considerably, so as to accommodate a new 'gridiron' and pits for the machinery. Everything above the stage worked on a German counterweight system installed by a Berlin machinist, F. Brandt, and everything below on the 'Sachs patent electrical bridge system'. The stage floor itself was rebuilt flat, with five great bridges which could be raised and lowered as required; the apron front was reduced, and the orchestra set closer to the curtain.

The Grand Opera Syndicate established a pattern which continued uneasily up to the post-war era of public subsidy, whereby a few wealthy opera-lovers underwrote the theatre's activities. Such small profits as were realized before the First World War evaporated thereafter. Between the wars, the Opera House fell into very low water. With the Covent Garden Market rampant as ever, it looked as though the theatre, 'badly located in an insalubrious neighbourhood, cramped in on all sides, and lacking such approaches as one would like to see associated with the Temple of Art'[18], would have to go. The freehold of both theatre and market twice changed hands in this period. First it passed to a family company controlled by Sir Thomas Beecham, and then to a less sympathetic property company. In 1933 it seemed that the writing was finally on the wall and the building would be demolished.

18 *The Builder*, 1 June 1901

48 The Stage at Covent Garden in the course of reconstruction, showing the electrical bridges being put in, April 1901

49 Edwin O. Sachs (1870-1919) the architect and electrical engineer responsible for the alterations of 1899-1901

Miraculously another set of patrons suddenly appeared, ardent enough to tolerate the juxtaposition of opera and old greens. Under this new Royal Opera House Company the building was renovated in 1933-4, some new staircases were made and an enlarged block of offices was built at the back along Mart Street. Further improvements took place in 1938, when the stalls were re-upholstered with a fleur-de-lys pattern. But the resurrection proved short, and in 1939 the theatre was again under threat.

This time the war was the saviour. Mecca Cafés now leased the building for the duration of hostilities as a *palais de danse*, installing a ballroom floor. After the war, the Covent Garden Opera Trust was established on the initiative of Boosey and Hawkes, and the Arts Council began its regular subsidies. With the performance of *The Sleeping Beauty* on 20 February 1946, the Royal Opera House began its present policy of combining seasons of subsidised opera and ballet. So far this has continued for 36 years, longer than any phase in the theatre's management since the eighteenth century. The security of this arrangement long depended on the good will of the freeholders, Covent Garden Properties Limited (later the English Property Corporation). Not until 1980 was the freehold of the theatre acquired by H.M. Government for the Royal Opera House, Covent Garden, and its future thereby finally assured.

Various changes have been made to the building since the present era began in 1946. In about 1950-1 the old carriageway was enclosed to make part of an enlarged foyer. In the summer of 1955 the whole of the stalls floor was taken up and relaid to a steeper rake to increase headroom in the orchestra pit, while rehearsal rooms and a canteen replaced a forest of wooden columns in the basement beneath. Finally, in 1964 the amphitheatre and gallery were reconstructed and united.

All these were small tasks compared to the great programme of expansion in the midst of which the Royal Opera House finds itself today. This plan goes back as far as 1965, when the Covent Garden Market decided to move, presenting the possibility of extra land, and with it new facilities. Various proposals were put forward, but all remained fluid until 1972. In that year the Royal Opera House received the approval to expand west to James Street and south to Russell Street, with the Government buying and placing in trust the necessary sites. The earliest phase of the programme began at the back of the theatre in 1979 with a large block of dressing rooms, rehearsal rooms and studios for both the ballet and the opera companies. This building, designed by GMW Partnership, was completed in 1982 and runs along the perimeter of James Street and Floral Street, where it is joined to the main theatre. Following a decision taken after prolonged debate, it

50 The auditorium in 1967

51 The amphitheatre in 1948 showing the division into Amphitheatre Stalls and Amphitheatre Gallery

carries on the simple stuccoed character of Barry's side elevations without material change. As a result, the Opera House now appears from Floral Street and James Street almost twice as large as before.

The timing and nature of many of the later stages of the expansion programme still remain under discussion and will be determined by the availability of funds. In the next phase, the new building will displace the extension of 1933-4 and be linked with the back of the existing stage to form a new rear stage. Along the north side of the Piazza east of James Street, a set of shops is planned with 'arts space' above. As for the site between the theatre and Russell Street, plans for this area remain uncertain for the time being, but it is sufficiently large for the provision of a substantial building, possibly to be shared between the Royal Opera House and other users. At the time of writing, therefore, the theatre finds itself in the throes of an expansion as ambitious as any in its august 250-year history.

The author of this chapter is to a large extent indebted to the account of the three Covent Garden Theatres which appears in Volume XXXV of *The Survey of London*. The author is most grateful to Dr F.H.W. Sheppard for permission to draw freely on this work.

52 Work in progress on the reconstruction of the amphitheatre in 1964

53 Work in progress on Phase I of the extension, 1981

54 HRH Prince Charles, with the Hon. Paul Channon, Minister for the Arts and Head Linkman Bill Bryson, unveiling a commemorative plaque outside the new Stage Door at the official opening of the extension to the Royal Opera House, 19 July 1982

55 Her Majesty's State Box at the Royal Italian Opera specially constructed for the Gala Performance of *Les Huguenots* on 20 July 1848

Gala performances have always afforded opportunities for the public display of royal patronage as well as the lavish decoration of the theatre. For Queen Victoria's State Visit to the Royal Italian Opera in 1848, a special Royal Box was constructed in the centre of the Grand Tier, lined with white satin and decorated with flowers, filigree gold ornaments and Brussels lace. In 1911 for the Coronation Gala, the theatre was decorated with 100,000 roses, the scent of which caused many ladies to faint. Since then, artists such as Rex Whistler, Oliver Messel, Carl Toms, James Bailey and Dennis Lennon have been responsible for the decoration of the house and for the accompanying gala programmes.

56 Her Majesty Queen Victoria and HRH Prince Albert in Her Majesty's retiring-room during a state visit to the Royal Italian Opera for a performance of *Il flauto magico*, 10 July 1851

57 Floral decorations for
the Gala Performance in
honour of the visit of the
King and Queen of
Denmark, 11 June 1907.
The programme
consisted of *Madama
Butterfly* Act I with
Emmy Destinn and
Enrico Caruso; *La
Bohème* Act I with Nellie
Melba and Caruso, and
Die Meistersinger Act III
with Anton Van Rooy
and Frieda Hempel

58   The Royal Box
designed by Oliver
Messel for the Gala
Performance of *Gloriana*
in honour of the
Coronation of Her
Majesty Queen
Elizabeth II, 8 June 1953

From Playhouse to Opera House

B.A. YOUNG

59 A political satire, *The Masque at the Old House*, showing the stage at Lincoln's Inn Fields, c. 1730

60 Engraving after William Hogarth of a scene from *The Beggar's Opera* at Lincoln's Inn Fields, 1728

The name of John Rich has a threefold claim to theatrical immortality. He put on the first production of *The Beggar's Opera* at his Lincoln's Inn Fields Theatre in 1728, when it had been turned down by Drury Lane. He was the most famous Harlequin of his day. And he built the first Theatre Royal, Covent Garden.

He was eccentric and ill-educated, but he knew how to pick actors – apart from himself. He longed to play tragedy, but was hopeless at it. On the other hand, he had a splendid talent for pantomime. He had taken over the Lincoln's Inn Fields Theatre from his father when that old rascal died. He built up a good company led by James Quin, acknowledged as the best actor of his day. To the classic drama, he added the special attraction of his pantomimes.

Rich inherited the Theatre Royal Patent from his father, who had bought it from the estate of Sir William Davenant, who had received it from Charles II. Without a patent, presenting a play in a theatre was illegal; although there were several theatres in London at the time, only two of them had patents, Drury Lane and Rich's theatre at Lincoln's Inn Fields. Largely through the success of *The Beggar's Opera*, Rich had boosted business at his own house to a point where he felt he should build himself a theatre that would rival Drury Lane.

The Duke of Bedford leased him a site in Covent Garden, and he commissioned Edward Shepherd, who had rebuilt Lincoln's Inn Fields for his father, to design the building. On 7 December 1732 it opened, amid immense ceremony, with *The Way of the World*, Quin playing Fainall. A Hogarth engraving shows the company entering in lavish procession, led by Rich in a carriage drawn by his actors.

The building of the new theatre had aroused a lot of interest, and the reception at its opening was friendly. 'The scenes were new and extremely well painted,' runs one account. 'All the decorations were suited to the grandeur and magnificence of the building.' The decorations were by Jacopo Amiconi, a Neapolitan artist lately arrived from Venice. Grandeur and magnificence were, however, confined to a small scale; from the front of the stage to the back of the boxes was only 51 feet, and the space allowed to each person less than two feet.

61 Ticket for the benefit performance for Thomas Walker (1698-1744), drawn by William Hogarth. Walker was the original MacHeath in *The Beggar's Opera* at Lincoln's Inn Fields

62 Lun (Rich) waves *Harlequin Horace* whilst assisting Punch to rid the Covent Garden stage of Poetry. The figures of Tragedy and Comedy stand on either side. Satirical engraving by G. Van der Gucht, 1759

The Beggar's Opera joined the mainly Shakespearian repertory on 16 December, the first musical piece ever played at Covent Garden. It had a run of twenty nights while the dramatic company played at Rich's other house in Lincoln's Inn Fields. John Rich made his first appearance the following January, as Harlequin in his own version of *The Cheats of Scapin*. Covent Garden soon became as popular for pantomime as Lincoln's Inn Fields; Rich, who played under the stage name of Lun, was as great a draw as the classic actors.
A contemporary rhyme said:

> Shakespeare, Rowe, Johnson now are all
>   undone,
> These are thy Triumphs, thy Exploits,
>   O Lun!

His career in pantomime had begun in 1717, when it was clear that he would never be a tragic actor. His pantomimes were based on the characters of the Italian *commedia dell'arte*, with plots that were fanciful versions of other tales. Harlequin might take any form. In a broadsheet called *Harlequin Horace*, we read that 'the ingenious Mr Rich deported himself very naturally in the Shape of a Dog, till a Dome rising voluntarily from under the Stage, gave him room for another transformation by standing on the Top of it in the guise of a Mercury.' Another writer describes him hatching from an egg: 'From the first chipping of the egg, his receiving of motion, his feeling of the ground, his standing upright, to his quick Harlequin trip round the empty shell, through the whole progression, every limb had its tongue and every motion its voice.'

Around these performances he devised a generous entertainment making use of mechanical stage effects (Rich was a handy mechanic). 'The "comic business" consisted of a dozen or more cleverly constructed scenes,' wrote the dramatist J.R. Planché, 'in which all the tricks and changes had a meaning and were introduced as contrivances to favour the escape of Harlequin and Columbine.' There was specially composed music that was designed to make a close commentary on the action.

The pantomimes were introduced to change the mood at more serious plays; 'we made use of them as crutches to our weakest plays,' said Cibber at Drury Lane; but this is an actor speaking – the pantomimes were as popular as the plays. As was the custom of the time, an

evening's entertainment might consist of a mixture of serious drama, pantomime, music and dance. Audiences never got tired of the familiar pieces, with their splendid scenery. For the whole of the thirty years that Rich was manager – and Harlequin – at Covent Garden, he had a repertory of only about twenty pantomimes, and of those, thirteen had come with him from Lincoln's Inn Fields.

On the serious side, the leading actor was James Quin, who had come with the company from Lincoln's Inn Fields. Tall and thick-set, he had a commanding voice, indeed a commanding manner that put everyone a little in awe of him. His style of performance belonged to the conventions of the time; he modelled himself on Booth, who modelled himself on Betterton, who modelled himself on Davenant, who was Shakespeare's godson. Speech was recitation rather than interpretation; movement led from one statuesque pose to another; emotion was expressed in a fortissimo.

The settings and costumes were as rigid as the playing. There is a picture of Quin as Coriolanus. A cloud of ostrich-feathers floats above his helmet; his tunic is teased into a wide frilled pannier reaching down to his knees. A curled wig hangs over his shoulders, buskins adorn his legs. This was strictly traditional; this is what a hero wore on the stage. The more important your part, and your position within the company, the more finery you might wear. The ladies might wear a gown in the current fashion, with the appropriate finery added.

In the spring of 1737 Prime Minister Walpole, tired of being mocked from the stage in the satires of Henry Fielding and others, introduced a bill – 10 Geo.II c.19 was its hateful name – that outlawed common players acting for hire, gain or reward where they had no legal right, and without a royal patent or licence from the Lord Chamberlain. So the unlicensed theatres at Goodman's Fields, Lincoln's Inn Fields (whose licence had gone to Covent Garden), the theatres in the Haymarket and all the theatres outside London were forced to close down.

Moreover the censorship, which had been mild where it had been imposed at all, was now reimposed with fresh vigour. Every script written had to be sent to a stage licenser at least two weeks before its scheduled presentation – and with the added insult of a reader's fee payable to the licenser.

You might think that with all the unlicensed houses closed, Drury Lane and Covent Garden would flourish. Not so. Playgoers, who had more influence on managers than playgoers today, disapproved automatically of whatever the Lord Chamberlain approved, so that the two licensed houses were compelled to keep to revivals of classic plays that the audiences knew.

In 1740 a new star brought the people flocking back into the theatre. This was Margaret Woffington, commonly known as Peg.

63 Peg Woffington (c1718-1760) made her Covent Garden debut on 6 November 1740 as Sylvia in *The Recruiting Officer* and immediately took the town by storm. So great was her success as Sir Harry Wildair in *The Constant Couple* that it was a long time before a male actor was again acceptable in the role

64 James Quin (1693-1766) as Coriolanus, 1749. Throughout his career, Quin refused to alter a single detail of his exaggerated costume

65 Peg Woffington's
first interview with John
Rich, 1740

She had been to London before, in an Irish
company presenting a teenage *Beggar's Opera*.
In this she played Macheath, Mrs Peachum and
Diana Trapes in the same performance. Now
twenty-two years old, she made a success in
Dublin with her Sir Harry Wildair in
Farquhar's *The Constant Couple* – not a travesty
part, but it suited her fancy. She called on Rich
at his house in Bloomsbury Square. He would
not see her; so she called again. She called
nineteen times before he received her. 'She was
as majestic as Juno,' Rich reported to Sir Joshua
Reynolds, 'as lovely as Venus, and as fresh and
charming as Hebe.' He engaged her at once.

She opened in November as Sylvia in *The
Recruiting Officer*, another part in which she
might wear breeches. Tall and dark, with the
striking eyes that were so often singled out for
special praise in those days of limited stage
lighting, she was an instant success. She
followed Sylvia with Wildair, which she played
for an amazing run of twenty nights. She played
several more comic parts that season and then
made the awful mistake of asking Rich for more
money. This was a favour he was not given to
granting, and Woffington crossed to Drury
Lane, where she stayed for the next seven years.
Her repute off the stage was as wide as on, for
she was a lady of notoriously loose morals. 'By
God, half the audience thinks me to be a man,'
she said once after playing Wildair. 'By God,
madam, the other half knows you to be a

woman,' Kitty Clive responded.

She was back at Covent Garden in 1748, and
save for a three-year break in Dublin she stayed
there the rest of her professional life. One
evening in 1757, when by her own uncertain
calculation she was 40, as she was speaking the
epilogue to *As You Like It*, she came to the lines
'If I were among you, I would kiss as many of
you as have beards that please me,' and
collapsed on the stage. She never acted again,
though she lived three years more.

Quin, who had been away from the company,
rejoined in the 1746-47 season. But now his old
unquestioned leadership had to meet a new
challenge for in the summer season of 1746 the
new young wonder David Garrick had crossed
over from Drury Lane, making his debut on
11 June 1746.

Garrick had made a lightning reputation,
largely by his Richard III at Goodman's Fields.
Inevitably both Covent Garden and Drury Lane
would be after him, and his first choice was for
the latter. He went there in 1742 – the year
when he set up house with Peg Woffington.
Drury Lane was in a bad way. Soon the
company rose in revolt against the manager, and
Garrick and Charles Macklin left with the idea
of forming a company of their own. This the
Lord Chamberlain would not have. Garrick (but
not Macklin) went back to Drury Lane, but
things were no better, and the manager lent him
to Covent Garden for a season.

66 The duel scene from *Miss in her Teens* written by David Garrick (1717-1779) for Covent Garden and first performed on 17 January 1747 with Elizabeth Hippisley as Biddy Belair, Garrick as Fribble, Hannah Pritchard as Mrs. Tag and Henry Woodward as Captain Flash. This is the earliest known print of a performance at Covent Garden

67 Spranger Barry (1719-1777) and Ann Barry (1734-1801) in Otway's *Venice Preserved*, one of the plays in which Spranger Barry appeared with Garrick at Drury Lane and which he first performed at Covent Garden on 21 December 1752, with Mrs Cibber as Belvidera

Garrick's acting was as different from Quin's as it is possible to imagine. No pompous recitation of the texts, in noble sculptural attitudes; Garrick's movements, his expressions, his inflections were meant to reflect those of life, not of crystallised theatrical characters. Such an approach was unheard of at the time; indeed, some time before, Macklin had been sacked · from Covent Garden for his refusal to put on what he called the 'hoity-toity voice'. With Quin and Garrick in the company together, some kind of conflict was inevitable.

In the event, it proved a very sporting match. Each played the roles they excelled in, Quin his Cato and his Falstaff, Garrick his Hamlet. Quin was well received in his old favourites, but it was tactless of him to play Richard III, for this was the part that had made Garrick's reputation. The house was half empty.

The climax came when both together played in Nicholas Rowe's *The Fair Penitent*, Garrick as the young Lothario, Quin as the solid husband Horatio. When Garrick came on to the stage, 'It seemed as if a whole century had been stepped over in a single scene,' the playwright Richard Cumberland reported.

'If the young fellow is right,' Quin said later, 'I and the rest of the players have been all wrong.' Nonetheless, Garrick and Quin became, and remained, good friends. If Quin and the rest of the players were indeed all wrong, Covent Garden continued to put up with it; at the end of their joint season in 1746-47, Garrick went back to Drury Lane, where he became manager and stayed for nearly thirty years.

There was another inter-actor duel in 1750, when Garrick played Romeo for twelve nights at Drury Lane while Spranger Barry played the part at Covent Garden. Barry, an Irishman, had a physical advantage, for he was tall and handsome while 'little Davy' was neither. 'Silver-tongued' Barry of the splendid voice excelled in young romantic parts, and the general feeling was that he had done as well as his rival in the contest (though Macklin, himself an actor of the Garrick type, complained that he swaggered and talked too loudly in the balcony scene).

Barry and Garrick had played together at Drury Lane, and there was no ill-feeling about the competition, which in fact was good for business at both houses. Gifted with a great natural dignity, it was said of Barry that his Lear was every inch a king, but Garrick's was every inch King Lear.

When George III came to the throne in 1760, Rich decided that this was the time to mount one of the processions for which he was renowned. It was to be an elaborate spectacle exactly counterfeiting the King's Coronation procession. Some of his actors were restive about taking part in an affair of this kind, which was not precisely what they were engaged for, so Rich announced that he would take part in it himself, representing the Queen's Chamberlain. At the final rehearsal, which did not take place until November 1761, he was taken ill. He died later that month, and the management of the theatre passed to his son-in-law John Beard, a singer.

Beard must be remembered with credit for his behaviour in the Fitzpatrick riots. Thaddeus Fitzpatrick, a man otherwise unknown, was determined to force the theatres to continue to admit the public at half-price at the end of the third act. He had already blackmailed Drury Lane into agreement, and now set his sights on Covent Garden. When Beard refused, Fitzpatrick and his gang of thugs smashed the place up, and Beard took him to court. He won his case, but this only led the gang to disrupt the spectacle with catcalls instead of damage. Beard finally gave in.

In 1767 the Patent was bought by a quadrumvirate – a playwright, an actor and two ambitious investors. They soon quarrelled with one another, and while their actions busied the courts, the management was undertaken solely by the playwright, George Colman, remembered now as part-author with Garrick of *The Clandestine Lover*. To him must go the credit for presenting Goldsmith's first play, *The Good-natured Man*, although he presented it without any enthusiasm. Garrick had seen it but made no move to produce it. It had ten performances in January 1768 and was coldly received; such homely comic inventions as bailiffs in the house were too 'low' for the public taste. The bailiffs were removed but success did not result.

68 John Quick (1748-1831) created the role of Tony Lumpkin in *She Stoops to Conquer* in 1773. He appeared mainly in comic roles at Covent Garden. In 1790, convinced of his ability to play tragedy, he appeared as Richard III for his benefit, to hilarious effect

69 *She Stoops to Conquer*, 15 March 1773 with Edward Shuter as Hardcastle, Jane Green as Mrs Hardcastle and John Quick as Tony Lumpkin

M.r Quick as Tony Lumpkin.

Goldsmith returned five years later with *She Stoops to Conquer*. Colman had sat on it so long that Goldsmith took it back and sent it to Garrick at Drury Lane. Then he wrote and asked for it back. In the end it was Samuel Johnson who persuaded Colman of its worth. On the opening night everyone half expected a flop, but it was a great success, and ran, on and off, for the rest of the season.

What had happened between 1768 and 1773 to cause this change of public taste? In fact, the change was not as sudden as that; it had been going on for some time. Even before Garrick threw his challenge at the formalised acting, its statuesque poses and 'theatric' speech, there had been those who believed that the theatre required more truth and less art. Macklin was before him, and it is thought that Garrick, who knew Macklin when he was still 'working' as a wine-merchant, may have got his ideas from him.

Charles Macklin, a talented but difficult actor, first won fame with his Shylock at Drury Lane. Shylock was always played as a clown, but Macklin dressed him as a Venetian Jew, with black gaberdine and red hat, and played him with the emotions proper to the part. Macklin even thought that Garrick sometimes overacted; he disliked his 'strange manner of dying and griping [sic] the carpet; his writhing, straining and agonising (all of which he has introduced into the profession of acting.)'

Macklin was not a regular member of the Covent Garden company, or indeed of any company. His famous Macbeth, in which he changed the traditional scarlet-and-gold military tunic for the costume of a Highland chieftain, was given at Covent Garden in 1773. And it was at Covent Garden that he gave his farewell performance, as Shylock, at the age of eighty-nine. It was clear to the cast that his mind was

SHYLOCK turnd MACBETH

70 Charles Macklin (c1700-1797) in his production of *Macbeth*, 23 October 1773

71 Note to the box-keeper from Thomas Harris (1738-1820), the manager responsible for presenting Sheridan's *The Rivals* on 17 January 1775

72 Richard Brinsley Sheridan (1751-1816) whose first play, *The Rivals*, was written for Covent Garden, as were the farce *St Patrick's Day; or, The Scheming Lieutenant*, and the comic opera *The Duenna*. Portrait by John Russell, 1788

adrift; but he came on stage, spoke the first few of his lines, then surrendered. He came down to the footlights, apologised to the house, and handed over his part to a fellow actor.

Because comedies that are still everyday fare began to appear at Covent Garden in those days, we must not think that the spectacle would be familiar to us. The stage, projecting into the auditorium beyond the proscenium arch, would hold not only actors but smart young men about town, an abuse not abolished at Covent Garden until the 1780s. Stage boxes on each side were upstage of the footlights. Upstage of them, at the base of the proscenium, were the doors by which most entrances and exits were made. The line of boxes continued round the house at stage level, with further lines above, and in the ring that they enclosed was the pit, where the public sat on lines of benches. Above the boxes was the gallery, except occasionally when hopeful managers did away with it – a certain cause of audience riot.

The scenery would consist of flats, beautifully painted, slid into position on grooves. A stereoscopic effect was obtained by putting a series of cut-out flats one behind the other. The wings might contain an additional face, at right-angles, sometimes including additional doors for entrances. Lighting was, of course, by candles. There was a row of footlights downstage, masked from the pit, and batteries of lamps in chandeliers beyond the proscenium and in the wings. The house-lights would be on throughout the performance.

If Colman as manager of Covent Garden can be remembered with credit for *She Stoops to Conquer*, Thomas Harris, his successor, must have similar credit for *The Rivals*, by the twenty-four-year-old Sheridan, who in the same season produced *St Patrick's Day, or The Scheming Lieutenant*. *The Rivals* was not

well liked on its first night; Sheridan blamed the actors, but more experienced critics claimed it was not to the popular taste. There was a change of cast, and evidently a change of popular taste, for the houses steadily improved. Sheridan at all events must have done well, for at the end of the season he crossed the road and bought part of Garrick's share in the Drury Lane patent. There he was installed as manager.

The next great name at Covent Garden was to be Kemble. Indeed there was a series of Kembles. The first of them was Mrs Siddons, who played Belvidera in *Venice Preserved* in February 1786, at a benefit for a friend.

She was the eldest of the eight surviving children of Roger Kemble, who had progressed from hairdressing to the running of a troupe of strolling players. His wife and all his children played in it. When Sarah fell in love with William Siddons, one of the actors, her father fired her. She went into service with an aristocratic lady for two years, but she did not lose touch with Siddons. Once they were married, they went on the road together, taking engagements where they could. She played at Drury Lane under Garrick in 1775, and was a failure. She reappeared seven years later, a more mature actress, and became an instant success.

Her brother John Philip was intended by their father for the Church, and after leaving school was sent to Douai College. He ran away in his determination to join the family profession. In 1783, he had an immediate triumph with his Hamlet at Drury Lane. Like Garrick, he introduced a manner of playing that was all his own, no longer relaxed and human, but serious and formal. He was well liked in tragedy but less so in comedy. A contemporary wit wrote his epitaph:

> Whene'er he tries the easy and the gay,
> Judgment, not genius, marks the cold essay.

A series of convenient deaths and retirements led to his appointment as manager at Drury Lane, but Sheridan's casual ways were too much for him. In April 1803, the unchallenged leading actor of the day, he bought a share in Covent Garden and became manager. He had the theatre redecorated, and added sixteen private boxes. He made his first appearance there, as Hamlet, in September. Mrs Siddons joined him three days later in the name part of *Isabella, or The Fatal Marriage* by Garrick and Southerne.

Kemble impressed the company with his tact. George Frederick Cooke, an able player when sober, was playing the leads. People assumed that Kemble would take over his parts, but instead of that, they played side by side on equal terms throughout the season. He was less discreet at rehearsals; in his Drury Lane days, an actor who resented his manner challenged him to a duel, and once he had to make a public apology for attacking an actress in her dressing-room. Black Jack, they called him.

He was no more tactful than his contemporaries with Shakespeare's texts: they were edited and rewritten, as was the custom, to please himself. He ignored the improved taste in costume that Macklin had initiated with his Macbeth; Kemble's Macbeth went back to scarlet and gold and a plume of feathers. (One night Sir Walter Scott cut it off with a pair of scissors and replaced it with an eagle's pinion.) The handsome scenery was as likely to present Bond Street for *Julius Caesar* as ancient Rome.

On the other hand, his devotion to Shakespeare – his Shakespeare – led to productions of much splendour, thoroughly rehearsed; even after his public adulation began to fade, there were still plenty who admired his playing; and the disasters that met him in the first years of his management cannot be attributed to him.

One of Kemble's early successes was the extraordinary phenomenon of Master Betty, the 'Infant Roscius'. At thirteen years old, he descended on London to play the classic parts at

73 George Frederick Cooke (1756-1812) made his debut at Covent Garden on 31 October 1800 as Richard III which, together with Iago, was one of his most successful roles

74 William Henry West (Master) Betty (1791-1874) as Young Norval in *Douglas* by the Rev. John Home. Master Betty, the Infant Roscius, made his debut at Covent Garden on 1 December 1804 as Achmet in Brown's *Barbarossa*, to immense acclaim. His fame was short-lived however, and he retired at the age of sixteen

75 John Philip Kemble (1757-1823), from a drawing by Sir Thomas Lawrence: the last likeness ever taken

76 John Philip Kemble as Shylock, 1809

77 J.P. Kemble came to Covent Garden in 1803 as actor and joint-manager bringing with him his sister, Sarah Siddons, and two of his many acting brothers, Charles and Stephen. Charles Kemble was also manager at Covent Garden whilst Stephen's greatest claim to fame was being able to play Falstaff without any padding. The family are seen here in *Henry VIII*, with Sarah Siddons as Queen Katharine, J.P. Kemble as Wolsey, Charles as Cromwell and Stephen as Henry VIII.

KEMBLE in SHYLOCK. "I'll have my Bond."

the great playhouses. The secret of his fame is hard to deduce. He acted in the sing-song, reciting, posing style fashionable half a century earlier. What people wanted was simply to see a boy playing men's parts, and they wanted it very much. Takings at the theatre were doubled. Parliament rose so that Honorable Members might see the Infant Roscius. While he remained in fashion – a matter of months – the Kembles withdrew.

Whatever the quality of the performances, there was no doubt about the profits. Kemble tried the same game again the following season, and offered an eight–year–old actress called Miss Mudie. She was hissed off. Juvenile prodigies having been put in their place, the way was clear for the Kembles to continue their reign. However, in 1806 a prodigy of a more lasting character appeared. This was Joseph Grimaldi the clown.

Grimaldi restored to the Covent Garden pantomime the reputation it had enjoyed in Rich's day of having the best clown in the business. His nickname 'Joey' has become the traditional name for clowns ever since. He was the son of a ballet-master, and began his life on the stage at two years and a few odd months. On Boxing Day 1806, he opened in *Harlequin and Mother Goose or The Golden Egg*, a new pantomime written for him by Thomas Dibdin. Grimaldi was not the romantic Harlequin that Rich had played, for ever seeking after his Columbine. He was a playfully wicked clown in the style of Autolycus in *The Winter's Tale*, happily deceiving his friends and picking their pockets. His own special joke was to turn various unlikely items into some familiar object.

He was an agile dancer and a popular singer, with a song called 'Hot Codlins' that was kept in the Covent Garden pantomimes for years after he retired in 1823, exhausted by hard work. It is

78 Joseph Grimaldi (1778–1837) as Clown in the pantomime *Harlequin and The Sylph of the Oak; Or, The Blind Beggar of Bethnal Green*, 26 December 1816

sad to recall that the theatre declined to give him a benefit. Drury Lane, however, from whom he had parted in anger, stepped in and gave him one.

Kemble's five successful seasons were brought to a disastrous close when, in the early morning of 20 September 1808, the theatre was burnt to the ground. It is thought that some wadding from a gun fired during the previous night's performance (Sheridan's play *Pizarro* with music by Michael Kelly) was left smouldering. The theatre and all its contents were destroyed – scenery, props and wardrobe, opera scores, pictures, the organ that Handel had left to Rich in his will – and twenty-five lives lost.

Rebuilding began at once, to a new design by the architect Sir Robert Smirke, and within a year of the disaster, the new theatre opened.

To recoup something of the loss caused by the fire, Kemble slightly raised the price of the

79 Playbill for the last night of the first Theatre Royal, Covent Garden, 19 September 1808

Theatre Royal, Covent-Garden.

This present MONDAY, Sept. 19, 1808,
Will be acted the Play of

PIZARRO.

The Musick composed by Mr. KELLY.

PERUVIANS.

Ataliba by Mr. MURRAY,   Rolla by Mr. KEMBLE,   Fernando by Miss PRICE,
Orozembo, Mr CHAPMAN,   Huaspa by Mr. BLANCHARD
Topac by Miss M. Bristow,   Huscah by Mr. Jefferies,
Orano, Mr. THOMPSON,   Harin, Mr. LOUIS,   Capal, Mr SARJANT,   Rima Mr WILDE,
Cora by Mrs. H. JOHNSTON,
(Being her first appearance in that character.)
Zuluga by Mrs BOLOGNA.

Priests, Virgins, Matrons, in the
TEMPLE OF THE SUN.

High Priest by Mr. BELLAMY,

Mess. T. Blanchard, Burden, Denman, Everard, Fairclough, King, Lambert, Lee, Linton, Odwell
Smalley, Street, Taylor, Terry, Tett, Treby, Williams—Mesdames Benfon, L. Bologna, Bolton,
Bristow, Cox, Cranfield, De Camp, Fawcett, Findlay, Follett, Grimaldi, Hagemann, Iliff, Leferve
Liston, Martyr, Masters, Meadows, Price, Ridgway, Watts, Whitmore.

SPANIARDS.

Pizarro by Mr. POPE,   Alonzo by Mr. C. KEMBLE,   Las Casas by Mr. CRESWELL.
Almagro by Mr. DAVENPORT,   Davila by Mr MENAGE,   Gonzalo by Mr. ATKINS
Valverde by Mr. CLAREMONT,   Gomez by Mr. FIELD,   Pedro, Mr HOLLAND,
Sancho Mr Brown,   Bernal Mr Powers,   Pablo Mr W. Murray,   Sentinel Mr. EMERY.
Elvira by Mrs. SIDDONS.
To which will be added *(4th time)* the last new Farce called The

Portrait of Cervantes;
Or, The PLOTTING LOVERS.

Murillo by Mr. MUNDEN,
Don Carlos Merida by Mr. JONES,
Don Guzman by Mr. BRUNTON,   Scipio by Mr. BLANCHARD,
Sancho by Mr. LISTON,   Father Benito by Mr. WADDY,
Alguazils, Mess. Holland, Brown, Grant, Heath, Sarjant.
Lucetta by Mrs. GIBBS,
Isabella by Miss BRISTOW.

Printed by R. Macleish, 2, Bow-street.   Vivant Rex & Regina.

On Wednesday, the Comick Opera of
The ENGLISH FLEET in 1342.
Count de Mountfort, Mr. TAYLOR,   Capt. Fitzwater, Mr. INCLEDON,
Philip, Mr. BLANCHARD,   Valentine, Mr. BELLAMY,   Mainmast, Mr. MUNDEN,
Katharine, Mrs. DICKONS,   Isabel, Miss BOLTON.
To which will be added the Grand Serious Pantomime of
RAYMOND AND AGNES; or, The BLEEDING NUN.
On Friday, *Shakspeare's* Historical Play of
KING HENRY the EIGHTH.
Queen Katharine by Mrs. SIDDONS.
To which will be added the musical Farce of LOCK and KEY.
On account of the great overflow from every part of the Theatre on the night of opening,
Shakspeare's Tragedy of
MACBETH
will be repeated on Monday next.
Lady Macbeth by Mrs. SIDDONS.

seats. In the boxes, what had been a six-shilling seat for seventeen years (before which it had cost five shillings for sixty years) was now seven shillings. The pit went up from three-and-sixpence to four shillings. He also enclosed the gallery.

The theatre was to reopen with Kemble as Macbeth (followed by a 'musical entertainment' entitled *The Quaker*). The National Anthem was played, and Kemble came downstage to make an opening address. He was greeted not with congratulations but with a chorus of abuse and cat-calls. There were shouts, clearly rehearsed, of 'Old Prices!' There was an uproar of banging and stamping, and in case the message was not clear, posters were unrolled from the boxes and the pit. The play went on, but not a word was heard. Magistrates came and read the Riot Act. Constables were called in, and even soldiers, but the noise went on.

It went on, indeed, for almost two months. This was the celebrated phenomenon known to theatre history as the 'OP riots' – OP for Old Prices. Men wore tickets labelled OP on their hats and coats; women wore OP badges. A ritual called the OP Dance was executed in the pit, accompanied by bells, rattles and horns.

Finally Kemble had to give way. The old prices were restored; for good measure the row of private boxes that had been added in the new design was opened to the public, and the engagement of Madame Catalani, whose singing had been made a subsidiary matter of objection, was cancelled.

The riots ended as soon as the rioters' demands were met, and Kemble was able to continue his august career as the theatre's most admired player. Mrs Siddons came and gave her farewell (though not her last) performance on 29 June 1812, as Lady Macbeth. In due course Kemble gave his final performance in June 1817, as Coriolanus. 'He played the part as well as he ever did,' as Hazlitt reported, and then retired to live in France.

He transferred his holding to his younger brother Charles, also an actor, who became the theatre's manager and continued in that office until 1832, though with mixed success. In 1829 his daughter Fanny appeared as Juliet; she was an instant success. Her popularity rescued her father from financial ruin, but after a few years

she emigrated to America. The last of the Kembles was Fanny's sister, the singer Adelaide.

It was during Charles Kemble's management that there first came flashing across the stage the unique figure of Edmund Kean. He was already past his prime when he came to Covent Garden. A dissolute life had undermined his constitution, and by this time an evening's playing exhausted him. He came across from Drury Lane in 1827 to play Shylock, Richard III and Othello, his three greatest parts. Then he fell ill, apparently with tuberculosis.

Kean's playing was rehearsed to the smallest detail. Keats (not a regular theatregoer) wrote that he 'delivers himself up to the instant feeling, without a shadow of thought of anything else' but a more expert observer noted that at every performance he spoke his lines identically, in timing, pitch and intonation, as if he were reading them from a musical score. He was small, without particular grace, and his voice was said to be ugly in the upper range; yet when he was on stage he unfailingly commanded the scene. Contemporary writers speak of the power of his dark eyes. He had that rare ability of making himself appear a different size and shape at need.

80 Cartoon of J.P. Kemble and the OP Riots by George Cruikshank, 1809

81 Sarah Siddons (1755-1831) as Lady Macbeth, one of her great tragic roles

IS THIS A RATTLE WHICH I SEE BEFORE ME?

Yet he was not a useful influence in the theatre, being concerned only for himself. After the retirement of Kemble (whom he admired), he claimed, 'The throne is mine – no man in England can rob me of the character of the best English actor.' He took no interest in production or management, though for a while he had a holding in Drury Lane. Nor was he concerned with other players.

When he had sufficiently recovered, he went on a provincial tour, which would bring him more money than playing in London. Then he came back to Covent Garden to give Shylock and Othello. On 5 March 1833, he was to play the Moor to the Iago of his son Charles. He was clearly unwell; but, charged with hot brandy-and-water, he made a brave start. At the line, 'Villain, be sure thou prove my love a whore,' he collapsed into his son's arms and was carried from the stage. He died two months later.

82 Charles Kemble (1775-1854) as Macbeth

83 Edmund Kean (c.1787-1833) appeared regularly at Covent Garden from 1827 to 1833, specialising in villainous roles. Coleridge is reputed to have compared his acting to 'reading Shakespeare by flashes of lightning'

The next significant actor-manager was William Charles Macready. He joined the company in 1816, a young man of twenty-three. In 1819, when there had been an exodus of many of the senior players, Harris asked him to play Crookback. He was not keen; but Harris (acting as manager while Charles Kemble was away) forced him by putting his name on the bills. It was only two years since Kemble had gone. Kean was playing the part at Drury Lane. Macready put a vast amount of preparatory work into his performance, and was rewarded with a great ovation – so great that he was called to take a bow before the curtain at the end, a tribute never previously paid to any actor.

He added another of Kemble's parts, Coriolanus, to his repertoire, and had a like success. Then, revealing a hint of the character that would unfold later, he persuaded the management to let him put on an unknown play by a new writer, *Virginius* by Sheridan Knowles. It took him a month, from the time he received the script, to present the play, paying for the

84 Fanny Kemble (1809-1893) as Juliet, 1829

85 William Charles
Macready (1793-1873) as
Orestes in *The Distrest
Mother* by Ambrose
Philips

86 W.C. Macready and
Helen Faucit in Byron's
Werner, engraving from
portrait by Daniel
Maclise

costumes himself and rehearsing the company.
The gamble paid off, and once more he was well
received. At the end of the season, he was given
a benefit, for which he played Macbeth.

With the restlessness of youth, he left Covent
Garden and for fourteen years played either at
Drury Lane or on tour. Drury Lane's manager
was Alfred Bunn, a penny-pinching operator
who in 1833 became the manager of Covent
Garden as well. After Bunn had given Macready
some insultingly poor parts, Macready pushed
his way into the managerial office and punched
him in the face. He had to make a public
apology; but actually it won him a good deal of
popularity. Then he decided to put into action
the scheme he had considered for some time,
and take a theatre of his own. Bunn had handed
over Covent Garden to a Mr Osbaldiston, and
the house was in a poor way. Although
Macready offered his talent without his money,
the management welcomed him in.

While he played at the Haymarket, he
assembled his own company. It included
Samuel Phelps, later regarded as the
profession's best actor, and a lovely young
actress called Helen Faucit whose guardian
insisted on putting into her contract an absolute
choice of plays. (She became less difficult later
when she fell in love with Macready.)

In his two years as manager at Covent
Garden, Macready worked wonders. He set
himself to provide productions geared to
historical accuracy. He consulted an antiquary
for costumes and even consulted Count
d'Orsay's hatter for advice in a contemporary
play. His scheme with Shakespeare was to
illustrate the play's thought rather than provide
vehicles for acting. The first scene in his
Tempest, for example, showed the action on the
sinking ship but omitted most of the words. The
choruses in *Henry V* were spoken from a
podium, while paintings on a diorama showed
what was happening.

His rehearsals, carried on with a maximum of
argument and bad temper, were designed to get
a proper performance from every member of the
company, even the supers. The result (as no
doubt he wanted) was that everyone gave more
or less a Macready performance, replete with
Macready mannerisms, the 'catchings of the
breath and asthmatic gasps', as the *News and
Sunday Herald* called them.

His first season in 1837-38 began badly, and
was not helped by Phelps's departure after being
deliberately undercast by Macready. But things
picked up. Lytton's new *The Lady of Lyons* and
Knowles's *Woman's Wit* were both successful;
the beauty of the Shakespeare pieces was
admired.

87 Helen Faucit (1817-1898) as Julia in *The Hunchback* by Sheridan Knowles, the role in which she made her debut at Covent Garden on 15 February 1838

88 Priscilla Horton (1818-1895) as Ariel in Macready's production of *The Tempest*, 1838

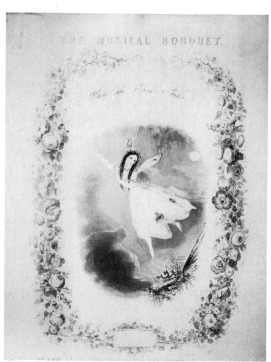

The theatre was a more handsome place than it had been in Kemble's day. The candles had been replaced by gas-lighting that could be dimmed or raised at will (Macready installed a new system). The public had been removed from the forestage. Macready commissioned splendid scenes from his scene-painter Stanfield, and elaborate effects from his machinist Bradwell, and he introduced new plays by the eminent men of letters who were his intimates. He was rewarded by a command from the young Queen Victoria for a performance of Byron's *Werner*, and it was not his fault that the audience was so unruly. At the end of his first season, he had produced 55 productions of Shakespeare, 154 other plays, and 138 evenings of opera and pantomime.

His second season, 1838-39, was another matter. His *Tempest* was immensely popular and played for fifty–five nights. *Hamlet, The Lady of Lyons* and *Othello* played weekly, and other plays old and new were slotted in. The pantomime, *Harlequin and Fair Rosamund*, was expected to be a failure. The dress rehearsal lasted over twelve hours, and Macready had to show the stagehands how to do their jobs. But it went well enough to play forty-one nights.

Two seasons were enough for Macready. He put everything he knew into his final production, *Henry V*, and when it was played on 10 June 1839, it was generously received. It played twenty-one nights, and on 16 July was the occasion of Macready's last appearance at the theatre. Four days later he was given a farewell dinner presided over by the Duke of Sussex, the first Patron of the Garrick Club. Macready's achievement can be seen by comparing the second season with the first. It contained 118 Shakespeare performances, 114 other plays, and only 79 operas and pantomimes. Shakespeare had achieved his proper summit.

Management of Covent Garden now passed into the hands of a husband-and-wife association. C.J. Mathews Jnr, a popular comic player, became the joint manager with Madame Vestris his wife. Vestris, known mostly for playing breeches parts in burlesque and vaudeville, was an unlikely figure to be found in that position. 'Her great celebrity rests on the beauty of her legs,' said one critic. She was a competent manager all the same, with ideas of her own about how to improve the spectacle.

She stepped off on the wrong beautiful foot, all the same, when she closed the shilling gallery for her first production, *Love's Labour's Lost*, and provoked a classic Covent Garden riot. She amended her error at once. But the first new play she offered, *Love*, by Sheridan Knowles, lost so much money that Mathews was plunged into financial chaos. However, a revival of *The Beggar's Opera* in its original costumes soon put things right, and *The Merry Wives of Windsor* that followed helped keep the wolf from the door.

The hit of the 1840-41 season was a new comedy by Lee Moreton, *London Assurance.* Mathews mischievously began a rumour that the play had been sent to Macready and refused; Macready, not a laughing man, demanded an apology, but no one knew who Lee Moreton was. He turned out to be the twenty–year–old Dion Boucicault, who obligingly signed an apology, though denying the whole thing. The play ran for sixty-one nights and made Boucicault the (to him) unheard-of sum of £300. Later in the season Vestris put on *A Midsummer Night's Dream* with all Mendelssohn's new incidental music, and this ran for fifty-nine nights.

But in spite of popular successes like these, Covent Garden was still being run at a loss. The debts of the Mathews–Vestris partnership mounted steadily, until at the end of their third season Charles Kemble and his partners seized the properties and the wardrobe, and Kemble

89 Playbill for the first performance of Dion Boucicault's *London Assurance*, 4 March 1841

90 Lucia Elizabeth (Madam) Vestris as Mrs Page in *The Merry Wives of Windsor* which she first performed at Covent Garden on 1 June 1826 for her benefit. Water-colour by Samuel Lover, c.1826

took the theatre over again. This was a pity, for Madame Vestris had sound ideas about the stage. She was particularly concerned with scenic realism. 'Drawing-rooms were fitted up like drawing-rooms,' Mathews explained. 'Two chairs no longer indicated that two persons were to sit down.' The sets of *London Assurance* contained, said the *Theatrical Observer*, not stage properties but bona fide realities. Vestris was a connoisseur, moreover, of a new style of comedy with small casts played by actors of more or less equal talent.

Neither of the two licensed houses was making any money at this time; the Theatre was going through one of its periodical slumps, and it was increasingly difficult for successive managements to balance the books. It was no help to them when in 1843 Parliament passed the Theatres Act, which repealed all the existing legislation and substituted a consolidated Act covering the whole question. It kept the old laws about censorship, which were relaxed only in 1968, but it did away with patents. Clearly the patent theatres without their monopoly were in for a thin time.

However, Charles Kemble took over at Covent Garden once more. He began with opera, a performance of *Norma* with his

THEATRE ROYAL
COVENT GARDEN
UNDER THE MANAGEMENT OF
Madame VESTRIS.

The **FREE LIST** (the Public Press excepted) will will be suspended This Evening.

This Evening, **THURSDAY**, March 4th, **1841**, WILL BE PRODUCED, FOR THE FIRST TIME,

A NEW COMEDY
IN FIVE ACTS,
ENTITLED

LONDON ASSURANCE

The Scenery by **Mr. GRIEVE, Mr. T. GRIEVE**, and **Mr. W. GRIEVE**
The Decorations and Appointments by **Mr. W. BRADWELL.**

Sir Harcourt Courtly, Bart.	Mr. W. FARREN,
Max Harkaway, Esq.	Mr. BARTLEY,
Mr. Charles Courtly,	Mr. ANDERSON,
Mr. Adolphus Spanker,	Mr. KEELEY,
Mr. Dazzle,	Mr. CHARLES MATHEWS,
Mark Meddle,	Mr. HARLEY,
Cool, Mr. BRINDAL,	Isaacs, Mr. W. H. PAYNE,
Martin, Mr. AYLIFFE,	Simpson, Mr. HONNER,
James, Mr. COLLETT,	Servants, Messrs. IRELAND & GARDINER,
Grace Harkaway, Madame VESTRIS,	
Lady Gay Spanker, Mrs. NISBETT.	

daughter in the lead, followed by an afterpiece called *Gertrude's Cherries*. He followed this with an all-star *Tempest*. Then he pulled out and handed over to Bunn. Bunn agreed to take control at Christmas 1843; until then the actors would run the house themselves. In the event, Bunn never came.

The theatre then became what is nowadays known as a conference centre. In September 1843 it was leased to the Anti Corn Law league. The following year, Daniel O'Connell had a full house for a speech made after his release from prison. In January 1845 there was a single performance of Sophocles' *Antigone* with music by Mendelssohn. In May the Anti Corn Law League was back with a three-week bazaar.

91 The Theatres Act of 1843, one of the contributing factors to Covent Garden's decline as a playhouse

ANNO SEXTO & SEPTIMO

VICTORIÆ REGINÆ.

****

C A P. LXVIII.

An Act for regulating Theatres.
[22d *August* 1843.]

WHEREAS it is expedient that the Laws now in force for regulating Theatres and Theatrical Performances be repealed, and other Provisions be enacted in their Stead : Be it enacted by the Queen's most Excellent Majesty, by and with the Advice and Consent of the Lords Spiritual and Temporal, and Commons, in this present Parliament assembled, and by the Authority of the same, That an Act passed in the Third Year of the Reign of King *James* the First, intituled *An Act to restrain the Abuses of Players*; and so much of an Act passed in the Tenth Year of the Reign of King *George* the Second for the more effectual preventing the unlawful playing of Interludes within the Precincts of the Two Universities in that Part of *Great Britain* called *England*, and the Places adjacent, as is now in force; and another Act passed in the Tenth Year of the Reign of King *George* the Second, intituled *An Act to explain and amend so much of an Act made in the Twelfth Year of the Reign of Queen* Anne, *intituled* 'An Act for reducing 'the Laws relating to Rogues, Vagabonds, Sturdy Beggars, and 'Vagrants into One Act of Parliament, and for the more effectual 'punishing such Rogues, Vagabonds, Sturdy Beggars, and Vagrants, 'and sending them whither they ought to be sent,' as relates to

Repeal of
3 Jac.1. c.21.

Part of
10 G.2. c.19.

10 G.2. c.28.

8 1   *common*

In 1846, Frederick Beale of the music publishers Cramer, Beale and Co was appointed both director and manager of a new company. Backed by the publishers and two partners named Persiani and Galletti, who could call on Rothschilds for £35,000, they were to promote Italian opera.

Nevertheless, the legitimate theatre continued to make sporadic appearances. The tradition of Christmas pantomime was maintained with credit; the 1879 *Jack and the Beanstalk* was described in *The Era* as 'the grandest show ever placed upon one of the finest stages in the world.' Sir John Martin Harvey liked the place; in 1912 he took it for two weeks for his production of *Oedipus Rex*, directed by Reinhardt. During the war it was used for charity performances. Then in 1919 Martin Harvey was back, first with his *Hamlet*, transferred from His Majesty's, then with *The Only Way*, his immortal adaptation of Dicken's *Tale of Two Cities*. It 'came of age' there, he said; its first night had been on 16 February 1889.

During several seasons, the theatre housed circuses. Occasionally, it served as a cinema. During the second world war it was used as a dance-hall for the troops. But really its destiny was sealed in 1846 when the builders moved in.

Covent Garden as a home for the drama was no more.

Plate 8 John Rich
(c1692-1761) as
Harlequin

Plate 9 Joseph Grimaldi
(1778-1837) in *Harlequin
and Mother Goose*, in
which he made his
pantomime debut at
Covent Garden,
29 December 1806

Plate 10 Edmund Kean
(c1787-1833) as
Richard III

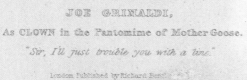

JOE GRIMALDI,

As CLOWN in the Pantomime of Mother Goose.

"Sir, I'll just trouble you with a line."

London. Published by Richard Bee

Plate 11 John Philip Kemble (1757-1823) confronted by OP rioters two months after the opening of the second Theatre Royal, Covent Garden

Plate 12 'The Balance of Theatrical Power for 1824' showing the continuing rivalry of the two Theatres Royal, Covent Garden and Drury Lane

Plate 13 Cartoon
lampooning
J.P. Kemble's attempts
to fill the theatre by
presenting lavish
spectacles at the
expense of Shakespeare and
'legitimate' drama

Plate 14 Mrs Johnston
(1782- ?), a member of
the equestrian company
in the melodrama of
Timour the Tartar,
29 April 1811

Mrs H-JOHNSTON, in the MELODRAMA of
TIMOUR the TARTAR.
Pubᵈ by Dighton. Spring Gardens, June, 1811.

Plate 15 A nineteenth century audience for tragedy

Plate 16 Set design by the Grieve family and assistants showing Dryburgh Abbey and Scott's tomb, for J.S. Knowle's masque *The Vision of the Bard*, 22 October 1832

92 The Great Anti-Corn
Law League Meeting in
Covent Garden Theatre,
1844

93 The Grand Banquet
to Mr. O'Connell given
at Covent Garden on 12
March 1844

Theatre-Royal, Covent-Garden,

This present WEDNESDAY, December 21, 1791,

Will be performed (not acted these Five Years) the Tragedy of

Tancred and Sigismunda.

Tancred by Mr. HOLMAN,

(Being his FIRST Appearance in that Character)

Siffridi by Mr. HULL,

Rodolpho by Mr. MACREADY,

Officer by Mr. EVATT,

And Osmond by Mr. FARREN,

Laura by Mrs. FAWCETT,

Sigismunda by Mrs. MERRY,

(Being her FIRST Appearance in that Character)

After which will be performed, a NEW PANTOMIME, (for the FIRST Time) called,

BLUE BEARD;

OR,

The FLIGHT of HARLEQUIN.

With entire NEW Music, Scenery, Machinery, Dresses and Decorations

THE PRINCIPAL CHARACTERS BY

Mr. BYRN,

Mr. FOLLETT, Mr. FARLEY, Mr. C. POWELL,

Mr. REES, Mr. MILBURNE, Mr. ROWSON,

Mr. Simmons, Mr. Blurton, Mr. Letteney, Master Webb,

Mrs. WATTS, Mrs. ROCK, Miss LESERVE,

Miss FRANCIS, Miss BURT, Mrs. ROCHFORD,

And Mademoiselle St. AMAND.

THE VOCAL PARTS BY

Mr. MUNDEN, Mr. FAWCETT,

Mr. DAVIES, Mr. MARSHALL,

Mr. Gray, Mr. Powel, Mr. Cross,

Miss STUART, Mrs. ARNOLD,

Mrs. MASTERS, Mrs. DAVENETT,

And Miss BARNETT.

The MUSIC composed by Mr. BAUMGARTEN.

The SCENES painted by Mr. RICHARDS, Mr. HODGINS, and Mr. PUGH,

Mr. WALMSLEY, and other Assistants.

BOOKS of the SONGS to be had at the THEATRE.

Nothing under FULL PRICE will be taken.

To-morrow, the Comedy of The CONSCIOUS LOVERS.

94 Playbill for the first production of *Blue Beard* at Covent Garden in 1791

95 *Harlequin Quicksilver; Or, Ye Gnome and Ye Devil*, 1805. 1/-coloured; 6d plain

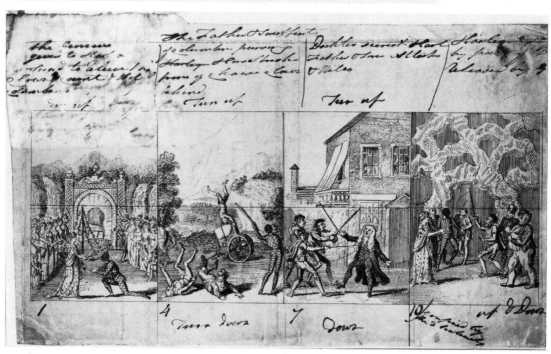

After which the Grand, Original Zoological, Comical Christmas Pantomine, by HENRY J. BYRON,

entitled HARLEQUIN

BEAUTY AND THE BEAST:

OR,

The GNOME QUEEN and the GOOD FAIRY.

The New and Extensive Scenery, Designed and Painted by Mr. William Callcott.

Assisted by Messrs. MORGAN, E. YARNOLD, W. WILSON, and WALLACE.
The Properties and Decorations by Mr. BRUNTON. Extensive Machinery by Mr. H. SLOMAN.
Costumes by Mrs. JAMES and Mr. COOMBES. The Incidental Dances arranged by Mr. W. H. PAYNE.
The Music composed and arranged by Mr. W. MONTGOMBERY,
The Pantomime arranged and produced under the superintendence of Mr. WILLIAM WEST.

BRUTINA (the Gnome Queen, resident in the centre of the Hartz Mountains, her native air, conse-
quently being "Hartz and Gnomes")... ... ... Mr. C. FENTON.
THE FAIRY SUNSHINE (the Good Fairy, the friend to harmony and I don't know how *many*)
Miss ELIZA ARDEN.
BRIGHT EYES AND BLUE EYES, the Attendant FAIR EYES   Misses DRING, TAYLOR.
PRINCE PERFECT, ⎰ (an upright youth, who eventually becomes a ⎱   Mrs. AYNSLEY COOK.
THE BEAST   ⎱   downright beast) ... ... ⎰
SQUIRE TIDDLYWINKS (a perfect father and a model farmer, a victim to a naughty
cultural propensity, who discovers, to his cost, that there is no rose without its
attendant thorn   ...   .   Mr. W. H. PAYNE.
MUDDLEHEAD (his own Man— "There is not through the wide world a *valet* so sweet."—*Moore.*
Mr. F. PAYNE.
FROWNINA AND SCOWLETTA (the Squire's eldest daughters, spinsters, who may be taken for
better, but [like the Author's rhymes] never for worse) MR. W. A. BARNES and MR FRIEND.
BEAUTY (the shades of all the celebrated bibliographers have been consulted in vain for an adequate
adjective—impossible ; suffice it to say that she is the Squire's youngest daughter, and, both
in property and personal attractions, takes very little after her sisters)
MISS LOUISE LAIDLAW.

COVENT GARDEN

96 Programme for
Beauty and the Beast,
23 January 1863

97 Scene from *Robinson
Crusoe*, December 1876.
The cast included a dog,
a 'live learned goat', a
parrot and an ape

GRAND PANTOMIMIC FANTASIA.
BLUE BEARD.

INTRODUCING,
THE FAVORITE AIRS MARCHES &c. PERFORMED EVERY EVENING IN THE CELEBRATED PANTOMIME OF
"BLUE BEARD" AT THE THEATRE ROYAL COVENT GARDEN.
ARRANGED BY
GILBERT H. BETJEMANN.

98 The Children's
Pantomime Party at
Covent Garden Theatre,
1871.

99 Blue Beard's Grand
Procession and Arrival
on his White Elephant,
from Henry J. Byron's
production of *Blue
Beard*, December 1871

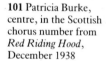
100 'Fairies suspended from wires, flying over the auditorium'. *Red Riding Hood*, December 1938

Pantomimes have played a continuous role in Covent Garden's history from John Rich's first appearances as Harlequin in January 1733 to the last performances of Francis Laidler's *Little Red Riding Hood* in January 1939. During his management, Rich developed pantomime as an art form in its own right and established a tradition for Christmas pantomimes at Covent Garden. Pantomimes flourished in the early nineteenth century with the appearances of Joey Grimaldi, the greatest clown in British theatrical history, and throughout the latter years of the nineteenth century, even when the theatre was in severe financial distress, the Christmas panto could always be relied on to fill the house.

101 Patricia Burke, centre, in the Scottish chorus number from *Red Riding Hood*, December 1938

1. One of the Arab Acrobats
2. Performance on the Slack Wire by Mdlle. Gisella
3. "Graceful Double Act on two Barebacked Horses by Jennie O'Brien and Mr. George Gilbert"
5. Miss Jennie O'Brien Fires a Rifle with Pigeons Perched upon it
4. Fraulein Eichlerette Exhibits her Troupe of Monkeys

THE CIRCUS AT COVENT GARDEN THEATRE

102 The Circus at Covent Garden, December 1886

103 Programme for William Holand's *Noah's Ark*, December 1893

—◦⊙ THIS PROGRAMME IS SUBJECT TO SLIGHT ALTERATION. ⊙◦—

1 OVERTURE, ... "La Cigale," ... ... *Audran and Caryll*

2 **MDLLES MARZELLA AND ROSE**
Their First Appearance in this Country
Flight of One Hundred Pigeons and Doves.

3 **COLLIER'S EXTRAORDINARY PERFORMING BULL**
A Wonder of Animal Training.

4 Professor **RICARDO**
will exhibit his Three Beautiful PERFORMING PANTHERS in their Cage.

5 SELECTION BY THE ORCHESTRA "Les Folies," (Polka) Cornet Solo, Mme. JOHNSON

6 **CLOWN REUBEN RUFFIN, and his Porcine Wonder**
AND JOCKEY MONKEY.

7 **PROFESSOR E. BONETTI**
Will show his Troupe of Educated
Foxes, Geese, Ducks, Fowls, Ravens & Dachshunds,
A performance never witnessed before in this country.

8 Mons. **W. PERMANE**
And his Five Performing SIBERIAN BEARS
Laughing Bears, Crying Bears, Talking Bears, Acrobatic Bears, Equilibrist Bears.

9 **HERR GRAIS**
will appear with his Riding
Baboon on the Bare-Backed Donkey,
PAT and **MIKE,**
acknowledged one of the most Marvellous Exhibitions of Animal Training ever seen.

10 INTERVAL OF TEN MINUTES.

11 SELECTION BY THE ORCHESTRA, "Lyric Gavotte," - - *Lila Clay*

12 **LEONI CLARKE, The Cat King**
And his 170 CATS, KITTENS, RATS, MICE, CANARIES, etc.
THE MUSICAL CATS play "Home Sweet Home," on the Sleigh Bells.
THE BOXING CATS. THE RATS' EXCURSION.
ONE HUNDRED RATS will start by Special Train on an Excursion Drawn by a real
Locomotive arriving at the Terminus the RATS take their Refreshment at the
Buffet, afterwards proceeding on their Excursion.
THE BALDWIN CAT will make a Descent from the Roof in a Parachute.
THE FUNNY CLOWN CATS.

13 **Mdlle. Nala Damajanti**
The Hindoo Princess, and her Magnificent
SNAKES, SERPENTS and BOA CONSTRICTORS.

14 **THE WRESTLING LION**
This splendid King of the Forest, in his cage, Wrestles with his Keeper, and goes through
some Startling Performances.

15 **EPH. THOMPSON'S MARVELLOUS ELEPHANTS**
Their first appearance in England. Trained Elephants have for years been seen, and some
have deservedly obtained great notoriety for the intelligence they have exhibited, but
never in the history of animal training have such exceptional performances been witnessed as
that given by these
Five Mammoth Elephants.
Among some of the extraordinary feats performed by these Wonders of the World may be
mentioned that two of these animals hold in their mouth a wire stretched across the stage, while
Madlle. Dolinda de la Plata
gives a thrilling performance on the
WIRE HELD BY THE ELEPHANTS.
Another Elephant plays the Sleigh Bells and a Piano to the accompaniment of the Full Orchestra.
The other Elephants give an astounding Acrobatic Display.

16 Mons. **NIVIN'S Marvellous Monkeys.**
JOCO Walks a Tight-Rope, his head enveloped in a sack, and Rides a Bicycle
on the Tight-Rope *à la* Blondin.
LOCO The Wonderful Flying Trapeze Monkey.
PETE gives an Extraordinary Performance on the Three Horizontal Bars.
The rest are Acrobatic Monkeys, together with the
FUNNY CLOWN MONKEY.

17 Lieutenant **CHARD**
Will introduce his CHAMPION DOGS.
The FINEST LEAPING DOGS and the FUNNIEST CLOWN DOGS in the PROFESSION

Those Two World-Renowned Eccentrics,

18 **COMICAL WALKER** and **FUNNY ALLEN**
Will Appear.

104 Martin Harvey as
Oedipus, January 1912

105 Lady Diana
Manners as Lady
Beatrice Fair and Cecil
Humphries as Walter
Roderick in *The Glorious
Adventure*, 1922.
Produced by J. Stewart
Blackton for the Stoll
Film Co. Ltd

106 Stacia
Napierkowska as
Antinea and Jean Angelo
as Le Capitaine
Morhange in the British
premiere of *L'Atlantide*
at the Royal Opera
House, February 1922.
Produced by Thalmar
and Company; directed
by Jacques Feyder

Dance at Covent Garden

MARY CLARKE AND CLEMENT CRISP

It is fitting that the theatre which has become the home of Britain's national ballet should, in its first incarnation, have called upon the services of one of the greatest dancers of the eighteenth century. Marie Sallé made her Covent Garden appearances under John Rich's management and he thus has the added distinction of being the theatre's first dance impresario. Celebrated initially as a harlequin, Rich was from the very start of his management eager to maintain the dance element in his entertainments in a theatre that was essentially a playhouse. His own performances and those of the dance troupes which were maintained at the theatre, suggest the importance of dancing even in a house less known for its choreographic programme than the Theatre Royal, Drury Lane, and the King's Theatre in the Haymarket.

The records so carefully collated in *The London Stage* convey the vitality of a tradition established under Rich's management and continued after his death. Hundreds of dances, including the social and popular dances of the period, hornpipes, country dances, minuets, 'character dances' concerned with some brief narrative incident, and those related to the dramatic situation in a play or opera, and the presence of a permanent dance troupe, indicate that in the main plays of the programme, as well as in the entr'actes and pantomimes which formed the afterpieces, dancing was of real significance and popularity. It is thus we learn that in the season 1760-61 Rich mounted eight new dances and featured dancing in 96% of the evenings that his theatre was open.

It was amidst this varied activity that Marie Sallé created her *Pigmalion* in 1734 in which the aspirations of the emergent narrative dance of the century were manifest. In simple costuming, without panniers and perruke, she proposed a truthfulness in dance which was to be the ideal of many of the forward-looking choreographers of the age. Yet *ballets d'action* of the kind foreshadowed by *Pigmalion* were less common on the Covent Garden bills than those shorter dances which were used to plump out the programmes and provide variety for a knowledgeable and keen audience.

With the turn of the nineteenth century, and the pre-Romantic era, ballet continued to feature in the entertainments at the Theatre Royal, Covent Garden. On 3 November 1820 came the first London performance of 'Monsieur D'Auberval's highly popular ballet called *La Fille mal gardée*' which, in a different guise, was later to become one of the glories of The Royal Ballet repertory. The dance offerings ranged over a wide variety of subjects. In 1823 the programme was 'to conclude with a revived and favourite melo-drama called *The Forest of Bondy or The Dog of Montargis* (in which Mr H Simpson's famous dog Carlo will appear). In Act I a Pastoral Ballet in which Mrs Vining and Miss Foote will introduce the Celebrated Dance from The Grand Romance of "Cherry and Fair Star" '.

In 1825 after a performance of the opera *Rob Roy Macgregor* on 31 October there was a 'New Comick Ballet, *The Shipwreck of Policinello*,' in which the celebrated dancer Mazurier, the darling of the Porte Saint Martin Theatre in Paris, made his first London appearance. He danced at Covent Garden for the next two months, also appearing in a popular dance melodrama of the time *Jocko, The Brazilian Monkey* and in a new ballet *The*

107 Marie Sallé (1707-56). This charming contemporary French engraving shows Sallé in day dress.

108 A playbill for the Theatre Royal showing the first London performance of Dauberval's *La Fille mal gardée*, 3 November 1820

Deserter of Naples choreographed by Austin, the house producer.

The great days of the Romantic ballet in London were hardly to touch Covent Garden Theatre, for it was Her Majesty's Theatre which, as in the eighteenth century, remained the major dance house of London. Nevertheless on 26 July 1832 Covent Garden was to show Marie Taglioni for the first time in London in the ballet which immortalised her, *La Sylphide*. The sublime Taglioni had already appeared in the city, but this Covent Garden visit was to reveal the full effulgence of her artistry. The troupe was very much a Taglioni family affair, with Marie's brother Paul as the hero, James, and his wife, Amalia Galster, as Effie; while Pierre Laporte, the manager of the theatre, took the role of Madge. Ivor Guest's *The Romantic Ballet in London* records that the scenery was produced by the celebrated stage painting family of the Grieve Brothers and that the Schneitzhoeffer score was adapted by Laporte's 'young brother-in-law, Adolph Adam, the future composer of *Giselle*, whose name was joined with that of the original composer on the bills.'

Filippo Taglioni, choreographer of *La Sylphide* and Marie's father, also staged *The Revolt of the Harem* at Covent Garden in 1834, and during the 1840s the Royal Italian Opera, Covent Garden, was the setting for a series of ballets by the choreographers Albert, Giovanni Casati, Jean Baptiste Barrez, and Henri Desplaces, which enjoyed a temporary success. None has survived and such works as *Manon Lescaut* of 1847 or *Gitta La Ballerina* of 1865 are no more than names in theatrical records.

Various stars of the Romantic age were, however, to be seen at Covent Garden, including Pauline Leroux between 1832 and 1834, and Adeline Plunkett, who arrived in 1845 with the visiting company of the Brussels Grand Opera and danced in the divertissement in Auber's *Les Diamants de la Couronne*. In 1847 Fanny Elssler made her final London appearance at Covent Garden, and Flora Fabbri and Sophia Fuoco also danced there. In 1848 the tradition of including a divertissement after certain operas brought Lucile Grahn to dance in *Flore et Zéphyr* following a performance of *Les Huguenots* in July, and the return of Adeline Plunkett. In 1852 the St Petersburg ballerina Yelena Andreyanova was also seen at Covent Garden; a lesser star, Madame Lecomte, danced in the 1840s in Auber's opera *The Maid of Cashmere* and also in the creation by Oscar Byre, the resident ballet master, of various *ballets d'action* including an extraordinary tale of brigands, *Hans of Iceland*.

Plate 17 Marie Taglioni (1804-84), one of the great ballerinas of the Romantic era

Plate 18 Skepsis, King of the Gnomes, and Pragma, his Queen, visit the cavern of the octopus, scene five of *Babil and Bijou*, 29 August 1872

Plate 19 Poster for 'the most amusing ball of the year' to be held at the Royal Opera House, December 1929

Plate 20 Margot Fonteyn and Robert Helpmann in the vision scene from *The Sleeping Beauty*, 20 February 1946, the production that reopened the Royal Opera House after the Second World War

Plate 21 Margot Fonteyn and Rudolf Nureyev in the title roles of *Marguerite and Armand*, 12 March 1963, created for them by Frederick Ashton and designed by Cecil Beaton

Plate 22 Julian Hosking, Jennifer Penney and Wayne Eagling in MacMillan's *Gloria*, 13 March 1980, inspired by the war-time writings of Vera Brittain

Plate 23 Nadia Nerina and David Blair as Lise and Colas, the roles they created in Ashton's *La Fille mal gardée*, 28 January 1964. The designs were by Osbert Lancaster

Plate 24 Galina Samsova and David Ashmole as Odile and Prince Siegfried in *Swan Lake*, mounted for Sadler's Wells Royal Ballet by Peter Wright, 27 November 1981

109 Scene from *Une Etoile*, a new 'Divertissement of a very gay and sparkling character' in which the action 'is carried on through a variety of choreographic forms, as a grand Pas de Fascination, a Bacchanalian Waltz & c., by *Stella* and her sister Stars', June 1854. One of the many 'lost' ballets of the nineteenth century

110 Fanny Elssler (1810-84) in the costume for La Cachucha in *Le Diable Boîteux*, an engraving from *The Beauties of the Opera* published in Paris and London, 1845, which celebrated the most popular operas and ballets of the time

111 Caricature of Mrs Vining (*fl.*1827-33)

Mrs. Vining in Gustavus.

ODE TO MRS. VINING.

Sweet Mrs. V. whose splendid legs or hocks,
   Kick forth to fascinate th' apprentice lad;
And the coarse texture of whose *raven* locks,
   Drive the admiring gazer *ravin* mad.

How overpowering is thy lovely grin,
   Which over all thy face urbanely goes!
Beginning in the dimple on thy chin,
   And ending in the pimple on thy nose.

How gracefully your worsted ringlets curl,
   Over a cheek adorned with patent red!
How very prettily your neck you twirl,
   O'er stuccoed with a coat of whitest lead!

When on thy tortuous capering I gaze,
   And see thy form with fatter nymphs entwining.
I get into a most terrific maze,
   Why you're engaged, *is* beyond my *di-Vining.*

The decline of ballet as a theatrical spectacle — and a diminishing interest in dance performances by mid-century — was a sad fact. Yet in 1855 Fanny Cerrito, then nearing the end of her career, was lured to Covent Garden by Frederick Gye to dance in *Eva*, a new ballet by Henri Desplaces. Queen Victoria, who loved ballet, returned to Covent Garden eight times to see Cerrito, and a programme change also brought a revival of *La Vivandière*, in which Fanny and her one-time husband and partner Arthur Saint Léon had delighted London a decade before. Gye engaged Cerrito for the summer of the following year but the destruction of the second Covent Garden Theatre meant that her farewell performances in London took place at the Italian Opera at the Lyceum in 1856 and 1857.

If the balletic contributions to the Opera House programmes in the latter part of the nineteenth century were to amount at best to short ballets after the operas – such as the 'new ballet of action' called *The Ambuscade* which was performed after Loder's romantic opera *The Night Dancers* in November 1860 – Covent Garden did provide a home for one of the most extraordinary spectacles seen in London during the Victorian era. This was 'The New Fantastic Musical Drama in 18 Spectacular Scenes' *Babil and Bijou*, first produced on 29 August 1872. It was the brainchild of the Earl of Londesborough, an enormously wealthy patron

of the arts, who hired Covent Garden and invited the playwright Dion Boucicault to write 'the greatest spectacle' to be seen on any stage. With lyrics by J.R. Planché, music by four composers, an action which ranged from 'The Silver City of Atlantis' to the middle of the air, and lasting for four and a half hours, the staging ran triumphantly for six months but yet managed to lose Londesborough £11,000 and gained dubious réclame as the most costly West End failure of the nineteenth century. Among its epic forces was a ballet troupe, and the 'Grand Ballet' in its ninth scene brought the virtuoso ballerina Henriette d'Or to London together with Léon Espinosa and supporting dancers.

As the nineteenth century progressed and London's ballet sank further into the decline that followed the great days of Jules Perrot's residence (1842-48), the art was to be banished to the music hall and the dance scenes in operas. Nevertheless the new Covent Garden Theatre would see many illustrious dancers, albeit appearing only in operatic performances. In the season 1878-79 the prospectus for the opera season included among its 'principal danseuses' Mademoiselle Zucchi, and it indicated that the ballet master was Joseph Hansen. Virginia Zucchi was one of the most exceptional artists in the ballet of her time, a dramatic ballerina of profound gifts and influence – her artistry during her Russian seasons in 1885 and 1887 was crucial in inspiring a new popularity for ballet. Her influence extended to dancers like M.F. Kshessinskaya and to artists like Alexandre Benois, whose *Memoirs* are testimony to her greatness. Her performances fired the imagination of the young Benois; in his turn he educated the young Sergey Diaghilev and communicated to him that enthusiasm for ballet which was so radically to affect the whole history of dancing in the West.

At Covent Garden, alas, Zucchi would be employed only in the ballet scenes in such operas as *Le Prophète*, *Hamlet* by Ambroise Thomas, and Massenet's *Le Roi de Lahore*, though Hansen did create a small ballet divertissement to show off something of Zucchi's charms.

The popularity of social dancing meant that many theatres in the eighteenth and nineteenth centuries were to be used during part of the year for public dances. The Paris Opéra was famous for the extravagance and sometimes licence of these assemblies, and in London masquerades and public balls were prevalent. Covent Garden Theatre was also to be part of this tradition, and the dance mania of the Victorian era, when social dancing – particularly the Polka and the Waltz – was to become widespread, led to a

112 Fanny Cerrito (1817-1909) and Arthur St Léon (1821-70) in *La Fille de marbre*. St Léon was Cerrito's regular partner from 1843 and in 1845 they married. The marriage and the partnership survived only until 1851

succession of *bals masqués*. Typical is this puff from *The Times* of 23 December 1845 describing one of the *bals masqués* organized by Jullien, the conductor. 'Monsieur Jullien gave his Grand and Annual Bal Masqué, or Mascarade, last night at Covent Garden Theatre. The manner in which the Theatre was laid out, the elegance of the decoration, and the brilliancy of the illuminations, surpassed anything of this sort which has been produced even at this place, and under the same direction on any previous occasion....The whole of the Theatre was hung with canary coloured silk, trimmed with crimson velvet and fringes, and bordered with gold lace.' *The Satirist* for 28 December 1845 describing the same scene declared that there was 'a marked change in the character and tone of masquerading in England. All was orderly. No crowding, nor jostling, no coarse language; good humour appeared to reign everywhere.'

It is ironic to note, in view of the description given above, that the fire which was to destroy the second Covent Garden Theatre was due to negligence following a public dance when, against his better judgment, Frederick Gye allowed the American entertainer J.H. Anderson (who called himself 'the Wizard of the North') to end his season with a masked ball.

The public who attended this ball were of thoroughly dubious nature, and a contemporary account describes 'the boxes filled with drunken savages, with their feet sticking over the cushions, some of them eating the supper which they had procured from the saloon, and two thirds of the male portion of the audience with cigars in their mouths....A general air of melancholy pervaded the place; there were no extra lamps to illuminate the boarded pit; and the dingily dressed dancers capered in a forced and solemn manner to the music of a dreary band.' (A comment from the *London Illustrated Times*.)

The beginning of the twentieth century was to find a complete reassessment of the nature of ballet in the West thanks to the Diaghilev Russian seasons which began in Paris in 1909. By showing superb artists in thrilling choreography. dancing to fine scores against magnificent décor, Diaghilev and his associates reasserted the theatrical power of ballet and its artistic importance. The dominant image of 'the Russian Ballet' was born. But Russian dancers had started appearing in Western cities before the first Diaghilev season. In London, Anna Pavlova and Lydia Kyasht and their partners had appeared in music halls, and in the year of the first Diaghilev Paris visit it is interesting to record that Olga Preobrazhenska and Gyorgy Kyasht were to dance at Covent Garden in June in a Tchaikovsky divertissement of mingled numbers from *Swan Lake* and *The Nutcracker* as a postscript to performances of *La Bohème*.

It was two years after the initial Diaghilev seasons in Paris before the enterprise was seen in London. Its presence at Covent Garden was due to Sir Joseph Beecham and his son Thomas. The young Beecham had seen the Ballet Russes in Paris and realised that it should be presented in London. Plans for a season in 1910 failed for a variety of reasons, not least the death of the King, and in 1911 Beecham set about negotiating a contract with Diaghilev to come to Drury Lane where he also proposed showing the Metropolitan Opera Company from New York. The opening of Oscar Hammerstein's opera house in Kingsway – later to be the Stoll Theatre – caused Beecham to join forces with Covent Garden to present the Ballets Russes. The Coronation Season of 1911 gave London its first view, between 21 June and 31 July, of what was billed as The Imperial Russian Ballet, though the company was in fact now a permanent ensemble directed by Diaghilev. He had been forced into establishing this settled organization following Vaslav Nijinsky's dismissal from the Imperial Theatres – it was only thus that a worthy setting could be found for the great danseur's gifts. The Coronation Season at Covent Garden included opera and ballet and Diaghilev's dancers, led by Tamara Karsavina, Nijinsky and Adolf Bolm, opened with a programme comprising *Le Pavillon d'Armide*, *Le Carnaval* and the Polovtsian Dances from *Prince Igor*. On 26 June a spectacular gala, attended by King George V and Queen Mary, by the royal guests for the coronation, the diplomatic corps and the leaders of London society, showed the Gobelins scene from *Armide* and fragments from three operas. The ballet repertory for this first visit was completed by *Le Spectre de la rose*, *Les Sylphides*, *Cléopâtre* and *Schéhérazade*. Its success brought a return visit in autumn 1911 when, in addition to the repertory already shown, more traditional pieces were danced: *Giselle*, which opened the season on 16 October and featured Karsavina and Nijinsky; the Blue Bird pas de deux and the third act pas de deux from *The Sleeping Beauty;* and on 30 November an abridged *Swan Lake*. Anna Pavlova, already the darling of London from her performances at the Palace Theatre, danced in the Blue Bird pas de deux with Nijinsky, but her art was more properly seen in *Les Sylphides*, *Le Carnaval* and *Le Pavillon d'Armide*. Diaghilev also played an astute card by inviting the prima ballerina assoluta of the Imperial Theatres, Mathilde Kshessinskaya, to join the season. Her dancing, her superb jewels and clothing, her enchanting personality, as well

113 A music cover showing one of Jullien's *bals masqués* at Covent Garden in the 1840s

JULLIEN'S BAL MASQUE

114 The fire which destroyed Covent Garden theatre after a *bal masqué* in 1856

as her Imperial associations excited press and public alike. She was first seen in *The Sleeping Beauty* pas de deux with Nijinsky, and then appeared as Armida, but her geatest success was in *Swan Lake*, also with Nijinsky, in which Mischa Elman played the violin solo for the lakeside duet.

In the following year Diaghilev again returned to Covent Garden for a summer season bringing *The Firebird*, *Narcisse*, and *Thamar* as novelties. Thomas Beecham, whose symphony orchestra had been a superb accompaniment for all the ballet's performances up to now, conducted certain ballets. The Russian Ballet's final pre-war season at Covent Garden was in the spring of 1913 when *Petrushka*, *L'Après-midi d'un faune* and *Le Dieu bleu* were new to the repertory. In this same year Beecham broke with Covent Garden and for its later visits the Diaghilev company was to appear at Drury Lane and the Prince's Theatre (now the Shaftesbury). It was not until the summer of 1920 that Diaghilev returned to Covent Garden with a company and repertory very different from that of 1913. Léonide Massine's ballets were the novelties which excited public interest. *La Boutique Fantasque* and *Le Tricorne* had already been acclaimed in London at the Alhambra Theatre, but *Pulcinella*, *Le Chant du*

rossignol and the opera ballet *Le astuzie femminili* were given their first London performances. They were less to the public taste. Beecham already had financial problems and a request from Diaghilev for an interim payment precipitated a crisis which was eventually to lead to Beecham's bankruptcy and the cancellation of the ballet's final performance.

The Diaghilev troupe did not return to Covent Garden until its last London season in 1929. Nesta Macdonald in her valuable guide to Diaghilev's London seasons, *Diaghilev Observed* (1975), provides an illuminating quotation from an interview that Diaghilev gave to *The Observer* on 30 June 1929: 'I return to Covent Garden with the sentiment of great emotion, for it is here at the Commmand Performance in the year of King George's coronation, that my Russian Ballet made its first appearance in London'. Headed by Olga Spessivtseva, Lydia Sokolova, Alexandra Danilova, Felia Dubrovska and the young Alicia Markova, with George Balanchine, Anton Dolin, Serge Lifar and Leon Woizikowski, Diaghilev brought the strongest company he had had for years. London was to see Balanchine's *Apollo*, *Le Bal* and *The Prodigal Son*; Spessivtseva danced in *Swan Lake*; and the range of Diaghilev's achievement could be understood from the presence of

115 The artists of the Diaghilev company in the Gobelins tapestry scene from *Le Pavillon d'Armide* which was performed at the Coronation Gala of 1911

Les Sylphides and *L'Après-midi d'un faune*, *Petruska* and Massine's *Le Sacre du printemps*. On Monday 15 July there was a *répétition générale* of Lifar's first ballet *Le Renard* and the first performance of the eighteen year old Igor Markevitch's Piano Concerto. The final performance of the Ballets Russes at Covent Garden on 26 July was to be London's last sight of this phenomenon of the arts in the twentieth century. Within ten days, the company had dispersed on holiday after performances in France, and on 19 August 1929 Diaghilev died in Venice.

During the dreadful lull which followed the death of Diaghilev in 1929, and the dispersal of his Ballets Russes, interest in ballet was sustained in Britain by the subscription performances of the Camargo Society (which gave two Royal Galas at Covent Garden on 27 June and 29 June 1933, when the cast was headed by Lydia Lopokova, Markova, Dolin, Ninette de Valois and Frederick Ashton 'with the assistance of the Vic-Wells Ballet'); by Marie Rambert's Ballet Club; and by the first steps of the Vic-Wells Ballet at Sadler's Wells. However, the demand for 'Russian Ballet' was still very much apparent. A major Ballet Russe troupe was re-formed in Monte Carlo in 1932 and conquered London the following year at the

116 Vaslav Nijinsky (1888-1950) as the Spirit of the Rose in *Le Spectre de la rose*, 1911

117 *Les Sylphides* in the original Diaghilev staging with Tamara Karsavina (1885-1979) in the centre, 1911

Alhambra Theatre. For Covent Garden, an attempt to provide something of the Diaghilev ideal was the brief visit, 6-10 July 1931, of Ida Rubinstein and her artists for a 'season of drama and ballet' which brought *Le Martyre de Saint-Sébastian*, *La Dame aux camélias*, and ballets by Bronislava Nijinska including *Nocturne* and *Boléro*.

It was in 1934 that Colonel W. de Basil arrived at the Opera House with a company whose different names across the years, and changes of personnel, indicate something of the changing allegiances and struggles for power which marked the history of the post-Diaghilev Ballet Russe companies in this period. (De Basil's trump card was the continuing presence of Serge Grigoriev, régisseur to Diaghilev from 1909 to 1929, who safeguarded the old repertory until the disbanding of the de Basil troupe in 1952.)

118 Anna Pavlova (1881-1931), with Laurent Novikov (1888-1956), in *Le Reveil de Flore*, 1925, during one of the seasons that she gave with her own company at Covent Garden during the 1920s

119 Tamara Karsavina as the Firebird and Adolf Bolm (1884-1951) as Ivan Tsarevitch in *The Firebird*, Covent Garden, 1912

120 Serge Lifar as Apollo in the first production of Balanchine's *Apollon musagète* for the Diaghilev Ballet in 1928, seen at Covent Garden the following year: Lifar's beauty in this role speaks for itself

In 1934, for a two month visit, Alexandra Danilova, the baby ballerinas, Tatiana Riabouchinska, Tamara Toumanova and Irina Baronova (then in their early teens), Léonide Massine, Leon Woizikowski, Yurek Shabelevsky and David Lichine were seen in a tremendous repertory which included the staple Massine ballets, Balanchine works such as *Cotillon*, and some of the Diaghilev masterpieces.

A year later, the de Basil company returned for an even longer season, from 11 June to 24 24 August, and in 1936 the season was extended even further, 15 June-29 August, when London had the chance to see Massine's third symphonic ballet, *La Symphonie fantastique*, and Lubov Tchernicheva appeared in *Thamar*. There were two seasons in 1937, the first occupying the whole of July, the second, billed as the Coronation Season, playing through September and into October. Already the tensions within the Ballet Russe and the disagreements between the astute de Basil and his gentlemanly associate René Blum, with Léonide Massine as the vital choreographic figure, had produced an intolerable situation which led to a split between Blum and de Basil. It was to be resolved by a major re-aligning of forces in the following year.

121 Ida Rubinstein (1885-1960) with members of her company in *La Dame aux camélias*, 1931

The Bystander, July 31, 1935 No. 1650. Vol. CXXVII.

The BYSTANDER

COVENT GARDEN'S GLAMOROUS NIGHT

Danilova, Massine, and Baronova danced in the cabaret given by principal members of Colonel W. de Basil's company of the Ballets Russes at the supper on the stage of the Covent Garden Opera House, after the Jubilee performance last week. This superbly "staged" party was in aid of the Russian Red Cross and of a benevolent fund for the Russian Ballet Company. It was attended by the Prince of Wales and the Duke and Duchess of York. The lighted auditorium formed a remarkable and enchanting background to the dancing

122 Alexandra Danilova, Léonide Massine (1895-1979) and Irina Baronova performed a Russian dance as part of a cabaret given by members of the de Basil company at Covent Garden in the Jubilee summer of 1935. *The Bystander* gave excellent coverage to ballet in the 1930s

The end of 1937 was also to bring a Christmas season by the Polish Ballet, whose artistic director and principal choreographer was Bronislava Nijinska, while its principal male dancer was the dashing Czeslaw Konarski.

Despite wrangling and a lawsuit, a 'Season of Russian Ballet' did take place at Covent Garden from 20 June to 13 August 1938 given by a company which, though de Basil's name nowhere featured, was his Ballet Russe. On 12 July, half way through this season and not half a mile away, a new Ballet Russe de Monte Carlo, with Massine as its leader, and with Danilova, Markova, Toumanova, Mia Slavenska, Lifar and Frederic Franklin as it stars, opened at Drury Lane. This was the summer of the 'ballet war' as fans scurried between the two theatres to see different ballets by both companies on the same night.

By September of that year the Ballet Russe de Monte Carlo had crossed Bow Street to play an unopposed season at Covent Garden. This was this company's last visit to London, for a scheduled Covent Garden season in 1939, 4-16 September, was cancelled because of the outbreak of war.

The de Basil company, still without the Colonel's name in its billing, played at Covent Garden in June and July 1939, with Baronova, Riabouchinska, Dolin and Lichine as its principals. The company then moved to Australia and the Americas. Its return to Covent Garden in 1947 found it a sad shadow of its once glorious self.

With the outbreak of war, Covent Garden once again reverted to its intermittent role as a dance hall. The theatre was leased to Mecca Cafés who transformed the lower part of the house into a dance hall for servicemen and women. It was to remain immensely popular in this guise until 1945; the era was notable for the arrival of American troops who brought the Jitterbug craze to this country.

It was on 7 June 1945, after nearly five years of darkness, that Sadler's Wells Theatre reopened and six weeks later its resident ballet company, the Sadler's Wells Ballet, went back to this, its original home, for an eight week season. But it was very apparent that the company had outgrown both the facilities and the requirements of Sadler's Wells. In mid-November the company was to go to Germany for ten weeks touring for the armed forces and at the end of the Sadler's Wells season Ninette de Valois made a cautious announcement that the company hoped 'to be back in London early in the New Year'. Most people had a fairly shrewd idea where the company would be dancing in London in the future and a clue came from the promoters of Mecca Dancing who announced that ballroom dancing at the Royal Opera House, Covent Garden would cease on 20 October 1945.

It was stated that Covent Garden would in future be devoted to opera and ballet. Thus it was that the Sadler's Wells Ballet was invited to become the resident ballet company at Covent Garden. Its translation to the Opera House meant that the Sadler's Wells Ballet was making the next, crucial step on its journey towards not only national but eventual international status. Covent Garden offered a home in the heart of the capital, room for more dancers and a larger corps de ballet, for productions of the size and grandeur required for the proper presentation of the big classical ballets, and for an orchestra of Opera House dimensions.

The winter months of 1945-46 were spent in preparing the production that would open the Opera House. *The Sleeping Beauty*, which had been in the company's repertory since 1939, was to be re-designed by Oliver Messel at a then exceptional cost of more than £10,000. Every

123 This cover of *The Skating Times* shows one of the more unusual uses of the Royal Opera House when it played host to an ice show in 1937

124 The Opera House as a ballroom in the 1930s. This occasion was a dinner dance in aid of the Motor and Cycle Trades Benevolent Fund

125 & 126 A ticket issued to servicemen admitting them to dances at The Royal Opera House during the war, and a stern notice featured on the proscenium arch

drawback and post-war shortage was overcome and on 20 February 1946 the red and gold curtains parted on a production that seemed splendidly opulent after years of blackout and rationing. A packed house which included the Royal family, members of the Government and the Diplomatic corps and what Lord Keynes referred to as 'the ancient hens of glory' (and with a distinct smell of mothballs), saluted Margot Fonteyn and Robert Helpmann (who was both Carabosse and Prince Charming) in the leading roles and Constant Lambert in the orchestra pit. It was an unforgettable evening, and, as if to prove that the company was truly a classic repertory ensemble, the next night brought Pamela May as a noble Aurora and introduced to London its first Soviet dancer, the beautiful Violetta Prokhorova, who had married the Englishman Harold Elvin in Moscow and had been allowed to come to Britain. She danced the Blue Bird pas de deux with Alexis Rassine and her Bolshoy style afforded a first fascinating contrast with the English dance manner. *The Sleeping Beauty* played for a month, with Moira Shearer and Beryl Grey also appearing as Aurora. Thereafter the company moved into repertory with the Sadler's Wells productions expanding happily to the larger proportions of the Opera House stage and with new ballets (notably Ashton's *Symphonic Variations*) exploring its wide spaces.

This first season by the Sadler's Wells Ballet was to be extended several times and its eighteen and a half week span broke all previous records for ballet at Covent Garden. During the 131 performances there had been hardly an empty seat and it was estimated that over a quarter of a million people had been to the theatre and *The Sleeping Beauty* had been performed 78 times.

The year 1946 was also notable for the first foreign ballet company to visit Covent Garden after the war. Ballet Theatre, now known as American Ballet Theatre, opened there on 4 July – what better day? – with a programme of *Les Sylphides*, *Fancy Free*, the Black Swan pas de deux, and Mikhail Fokine's last ballet *Bluebeard*. The company was led by Alicia Alonso, Nora Kaye, André Eglevsky, Jerome Robbins and John Kriza and reminded the London public – as did that summer's appearances elsewhere in London by Roland Petit's Ballets des Champs Elysées, with Jean Babilée, and Lifar's Nouveau Ballet de Monte Carlo, with Yvette Chauviré – that there was a larger world of ballet to be admired and explored after six years of wartime deprivation.

One visitor to the Sadler's Wells company was to be of particular importance at this time. This was Léonide Massine. At the invitation of Ninette de Valois he staged *Le Tricorne* and *La Boutique Fantasque* in the spring of 1947, with the choreographer himself, agelessly brilliant and vivid, as the Miller and the Can–Can Dancer. With Fonteyn as the Miller's Wife and Moira Shearer as the other Can–Can Dancer the continuing vitality of these ballets was in marked contrast to the return of the de Basil company to Covent Garden in July 1947.

Billed as The Original Ballet Russe, the company was dreadfully thin despite the guiding presences of Serge Grigoriev and Lubov Tchernicheva and the participation of such exceptional artists as Tatiana Riabouchinska and David Lichine, Nicholas Orlov and Roman Jasinsky (while, of the new recruits, Renée Jeanmaire and Vladimir Skouratoff were dancers of superb calibre). But the sad fact was that the Sadler's Wells Ballet had taught the public to seek for different ballets and a different manner. The glamour of the Ballet Russe had faded irreparably, and four years later the de Basil troupe and its director were dead.

At the time when the Sadler's Wells Ballet was entering upon a period of remarkable expansion – Ashton's *Cinderella* in 1948 very significant as the first classic full length ballet produced by the company; its New York triumph in the following year, when *The Sleeping Beauty* conquered the Metropolitan Opera House audience, an indication of the company's new international status – Covent Garden was able also to present important guests. Alicia Markova and Anton Dolin returned to dance the classic repertory with the company during the summer of 1948 to immense acclaim, and were to return, individually, in subsequent years. They were followed in the spring of 1949 by Alexandra Danilova and Frederic Franklin who were seen in *Coppélia* and *Giselle*, while Danilova was joined by Massine for some glorious performances of *La Boutique Fantasque*.

In mid-July 1948 a staging of *The Pilgrim's Progress* as a dramatic/musical entertainment was seen at the Opera House for a short season, with a cast which included Svetlana Beriosova and the dancers of the Metropolitan Ballet. Then in August the Grand Ballet de Monte Carlo, later to be the Grand Ballet du Marquis de Cuevas, appeared, to hold high the banner of taste of its Maecenas, with Rosella Hightower and André Eglevsky, Marjorie Tallchief and George Skibine the stars of its first season. Unforgettable were performances of Balanchine's *Concerto Barocco* and *Night Shadow* (Skibine the ideal poet) and Lifar's *Noir et Blanc*, and the prodigies of virtuosity offered by Hightower and Eglevsky in the Black Swan duet. The de Cuevas company was to return in

the following year bringing Toumanova and
Massine, Riabouchinska and Lichine, as well as
ballets by Nijinska and the Massine/Dali
extravaganza *Mad Tristan*.

The decade of the 1950s was a glorious one
for the Sadler's Wells Ballet. In 1956, the year
of its silver jubilee, a Royal Charter was
bestowed upon the company, which could now
proudly call itself The Royal Ballet. Frederick
Ashton was producing a magnificent series of
ballets, which included the full length works
Sylvia and *Ondine*, and the choreography of the
new generation of creative artists produced
by the company, John Cranko and Kenneth
MacMillan, was making its mark. Both had
served an apprenticeship with the second
company – the Sadler's Wells Theatre Ballet –
and Cranko has crowned his achievements with
his first full-length work, *The Prince of the
Pagodas* with its commissioned Britten score,
while MacMillan has made his first two works at
the Opera House, *Agon* and *Noctambules*.

The tragedy of this decade had been the
untimely death of Constant Lambert. Our
national ballet owed to him its musical
standards, and his lively mind stimulated every
associate. In purely practical terms, the Opera
House years of the Sadler's Wells Ballet had
been illuminated by the theatrical glow of the
orchestral performances under Lambert's
baton. His death was the greatest loss our

127 Léonide Massine as
the Miller with Beryl
Grey (right) and Moira
Shearer in *Le Tricorne* as
staged for the Sadler's
Wells Ballet at Covent
Garden in 1947

128 Michael Kidd (left),
and Alicia Alonso as the
girl who auditions for a
ballet company in
Kidd's *On Stage!* with
members of Ballet
Theatre, 1946

national ballet was to know.

Covent Garden acknowledged its continuing duty to show foreign companies during the summer recess throughout the 1950s. The summer of 1950 was American, with the New York City Ballet making its first European appearance in a magnificent six week season, followed by a return of American Ballet Theatre, who were to be seen again in 1953 and 1956.

129 Alicia Markova and Anton Dolin in the last act pas de deux from *The Sleeping Beauty*. Markova and Dolin were seen for the first time in this full-length version when they returned to London as guests with the Sadler's Wells Ballet in 1948

130 Ethery Pagava and André Eglevsky in Léonide Massine's *Mad Tristan* as presented by the de Cuevas company at Covent Garden in 1949. The hallucinatory decor was by Salvador Dali

131 Alexandra Danilova and Frederic Franklin leaving a New York theatre at the end of an American season by the Ballet Russe de Monte Carlo before setting out for their London season with the Sadler's Wells Ballet in 1949

Two years later New York City Ballet again returned, and London was to have its last opportunity until 1966 to appreciate the stature of Balanchine's choreography and of his dancers. There followed three European companies to remind the London public of very different national styles of dancing. As Richard Buckle noted: 'At last, after two centuries, the Royal Danish Ballet has sallied forth from Scandinavia and advances as conqueror on London'. In the summer of 1953 the revelation of the Bournonville school and choreography and the splendour of the company, led by Margrethe Schanne, Erik Bruhn, Fredbjørn Bjørnsson, Gerda Karstens, Kirsten Ralov, Inge Sand, Mona Vangsaa, Frank Schaufuss and Niels Bjørn Larsen awoke London to the beauty of Danish dance and mime. In 1954 the Paris Opéra Ballet made a no less important visit. A superb company, led by Chauviré and Nina Vyroubova, Lifar, Youly Algaroff and Michel Renault in a repertory dominated by Lifar's choreography, was an opulent display of dance talent even if it was not fully appreciated by the London audience. One exotic and very powerful memory of this period comes from the appearance of the grand troupe of Azuma Kabuki Dancers and Musicians who appeared at the Opera House in 1955.

132 David Blair (1932-76) and Svetlana Beriosova in *The Prince of the Pagodas*, 1957

133 *Birthday Offering*, with its original cast. Margot Fonteyn and Michael Somes are in the centre. The other couples (left to right) are Elaine Fifield and Brian Shaw, Rowena Jackson and Desmond Doyle, Svetlana Beriosova and Bryan Ashbridge, Beryl Grey and Philip Chatfield, Violetta Elvin and David Blair, Nadia Nerina and Alexander Grant

134 Constant Lambert (1905-51). Chief conductor and musical director for the Sadler's Wells Ballet from 1931 to 1947

In 1956 there came that visit which can only be compared in importance with the first, revelatory Diaghilev season in Paris in 1909. Once again the excitement came from Russia, but this time it was Soviet ballet when, in October, the Moscow Bolshoy Ballet appeared at Covent Garden.

This first full season in the West was initially dogged by difficulties. These related to the arrest in London of Nina Ponomaryeva, a Soviet athlete, accused of stealing five hats (value 32s.11d) from C & A Modes at Marble Arch. 'Provocation' said *Izvestia*, but the diplomatic skill of David Webster, General Administrator of The Royal Opera House, won through. After six cliff-hanging days in September, the Bolshoy visit 'was on' as the *Evening Standard* front page headline said on 27 September. The Bolshoy company arrived only on 1 October, to vast publicity.

The season opened on 3 October with Galina Ulanova and Yury Zhdanov in Leonid Lavrovsky's *Romeo and Juliet*. The entire ballet world seemed to be watching – and the entire ballet world seemed to be present in the Opera House – as Ulanova and the Moscow company triumphed absolutely. The performances of the company in *Romeo and Juliet*, *The Fountain of Bakhchisaray*, and *Giselle* have passed into legend, as have the musical standards of the conductor, Yury Fayer. So have the queues which had wound down the side of the Opera House and even crossed Bow Street into Broad Court.

In 1961 the Opera House was again host for the first appearance of a great Russian company when the Leningrad State Kirov Ballet made its London debut. Here was the luminosity of moonlight as compared with the blazing sun of the Bolshoy. Led by Irina Kolpakova, who appeared as a sublime Aurora in an ideal *Sleeping Beauty*, with Alla Ossipenko, Inna Zubkovskaya and the young Natalia Makarova, who astounded London in *Giselle*, with Vladilen Semenov, Oleg Sokolov and the angelic Yury Solovyov who opened the season with the young Alla Sizova in *The Stone Flower*, the aristocracy and grandeur of the company's style and productions were for some observers even more

135 One of the most spectacular works brought by the Paris Opéra Ballet on its first visit to Covent Garden in 1954 was this scene from *Les Indes galantes*, Rameau's opera-ballet of 1735 which had been magnificently restaged in 1952. The flower scene was choreographed by Harald Lander and designed by Fost and Moulène

136 The forest scene in *Ondine*, Act I, with Margot Fonteyn held high above the water sprites, Michael Somes (left) as Palemon and Alexander Grant (right) as Tirrenio, 1958

thrilling than the Bolshoy. The missing figure was, of course, Rudolf Nureyev. He had left the Kirov in Paris and was not to arrive at Covent Garden until the following February when he partnered Fonteyn in *Giselle* and thus initiated their celebrated collaboration.

One other important 'visitor' to the Opera House must here be mentioned. In 1958 the touring section of The Royal Ballet came into Covent Garden for a first season bringing young dancers and young choreographers – works by

John Cranko, Peter Wright and Kenneth MacMillan were on view for the first time. Thereafter the company was to give regular and welcome guest seasons, occasionally with a stiffening of invited artists – the summer of 1963 brought Carla Fracci, Melissa Hayden, Belinda Wright, John Gilpin and Flemming Flindt – but the touring company soon proved its right to hold the stage on its own merits. Doreen Wells, David Wall, Christopher Gable, Elizabeth Anderton and Brenda Last were among the stars of the troupe who were adored throughout the country and soon became Covent Garden favourites. Although Sadler's Wells Royal Ballet, which does such invaluable touring work, is based on Sadler's Wells Theatre it too is seen in London to even better advantage when it moves up to Bow Street, its true home as a part of The Royal Ballet. The work of the two companies is complementary.

As a corollary to the work of The Royal Ballet there are also the performances given by the Royal Ballet School. In 1959 the first 'school matinee' was given at Covent Garden. This was a performance of *Coppélia* in which two young talents of The Royal Ballet took the principal roles – Antoinette Sibley and Graham Usher were Swanilda and Franz. In following years leading roles were assumed by students and the matinees became evening performances – even a

137 *Caracole* (revised as *Divertimento No 15* by the NYCB and taking its name from the Mozart score) was one of the most thrilling examples of Balanchine's work given in the New York City Ballet's second season of 1952. The dancers (left to right) are Jillana, Yvonne Mounsey, Patricia Wilde, Diana Adams and Melissa Hayden

138 Erik Bruhn as Junker Øve and Kirsten Ralov as Frøken Birthe (centre) with members of the Royal Danish Ballet in the first scene of Bournonville's *A Folk Tale* at Covent Garden, 1953

Plate 25 A new production of Ashton's *Cinderella*, 23 December 1965, with Frederick Ashton and Robert Helpmann as the Ugly Sisters

Plate 26 Laura Connor, Merle Park, Jennifer Penney and Michael Coleman in a revival of Ashton's *Symphonic Variations*, 1973

Plate 27 Kenneth MacMillan's *Rite of Spring*, 3 May 1962, with Monica Mason as the Chosen Maiden; designs by Sidney Nolan

Plate 28 Robert Helpmann as the Red King with Sadler's Wells Royal Ballet in a revival of de Valois's *Checkmate*, 1977

Plate 29 *Les Noces* mounted for The Royal Ballet in 1966 by Bronislava Nijinska. 1971 revival with Gerd Larsen as the Mother, Vergie Derman as the Bride and Christopher Newton as the Father

Plate 30 Sadler's Wells Royal Ballet in John Cranko's *Pineapple Poll*, 1979, with David Morse as Jasper, June Highwood as Miss Dimple, David Ashmole as Captain Belaye, and Christine Aitken as Blanche

Plate 31 The gambling scene from MacMillan's *Manon*, 7 March 1974, with David Adams as a Client, Antoinette Sibley as Manon, Derek Rencher as Monsieur G.M., David Wall as Lescaut and Anthony Dowell as Des Grieux

Plate 32 Margot Fonteyn as the Firebird in the production mounted for The Royal Ballet by Serge Grigoriev and Lubov Tchernicheva which was first given at the Edinburgh Festival on 23 August 1954 to commemorate the twenty-fifth anniversary of the death of Diaghilev

139 Alla Sizova as
Katerina and Yury
Solovyov (1940-77) as
Danila in *The Stone
Flower* by Yury
Grigorovich which
opened the Kirov season
in London, 1961

140 Galina Ulanova as
Juliet and Alexander
Lapauri as Paris in
Leonid Lavrovsky's
Romeo and Juliet which
so triumphantly opened
the first London season
of the Bolshoy Ballet at
Covent Garden, 1956

Royal Gala – and were followed by a full week of performances at another theatre. The Covent Garden performance, however, is the thrilling one, an opportunity for talent-spotting by the public, and for ebullient and endearing dancing by the members of both the Lower and Upper Schools.

The decade of the 1960s was important for The Royal Ballet at Covent Garden. In 1963 Dame Ninette de Valois announced her retirement as Director of The Royal Ballet. In thirty-two years she had moved from a group of six dancers in the newly-reopened Sadler's Wells Theatre to two companies and two schools (the junior one residential at White Lodge in Richmond Park), and the acknowledgement that Britain's national ballet was one of the greatest in the world. It was inevitable and right that she should be succeeded by Frederick Ashton, with Michael Somes, John Field and John Hart as assistant directors.

The company that Ashton inherited was a very strong one. He had endowed it with a series of major works, not least the wonderful *La Fille mal gardée* for Nadia Nerina, David Blair, Alexander Grant, Stanley Holden and Leslie Edwards, which had been first performed in 1960. In Kenneth MacMillan there was now a new choreographic voice whose achievements during this period were to culminate with *Romeo and Juliet* in 1965, and there were the illustrious figures of Fonteyn and Nureyev, Nerina, Svetlana Beriosova and Blair, and the new generation of artists headed by Antoinette Sibley and Anthony Dowell, whose partnership was to be so beautifully placed in Ashton's *The Dream*, Lynn Seymour and Christopher Gable (for whom MacMillan created *Romeo and Juliet*), Merle Park, Donald MacLeary, and Monica Mason whose gifts were so potently recognised in MacMillan's *Rite of Spring*.

Among Opera House visitors during this period both the Bolshoy and the Kirov returned, the Bolshoy in 1963 being led by Maya Plisetskaya in magnificent form in *Don Quixote*, *Romeo and Juliet*, and *The Little Hump-backed Horse*, and with Raissa Struchkova welcomed back to London, and the revelation of Vladimir Vasiliev, Ekaterina Maximova and Natalia Bessmertnova. The season was a great success. Alas, a third visit, six years later, proved a sad disappointment both in style and repertory. The Kirov also came back in the autumn of 1966, and again London could appreciate the company's glorious classic style. In 1965 the Commonwealth Festival brought the Australian Ballet briefly to the Opera House as part of a European tour, and that same year the New York City Ballet returned to London after too long an absence.

141 The first scene of Kenneth MacMillan's *The Invitation* with its original cast at Covent Garden, 1963. (Left to right) Lynn Seymour as the Girl, Christopher Gable as the Boy, and Desmond Doyle as the Husband

143 At the first performance given by the Royal Ballet School at Covent Garden, Antoinette Sibley and Graham Usher (1938-75), graduates of the School and then new members of The Royal Ballet, were seen as Swanilda and Franz, with the rest of the cast made up of students from the School. The production was that designed by Osbert Lancaster

142 Desmond Kelly as the Prodigal and June Highwood as The Siren in Balanchine's *The Prodigal Son* as presented by Sadler's Wells Royal Ballet, 1982

144 Doreen Wells as Sylvia and Christopher Gable as Aminta in the final pas de deux of Ashton's *Sylvia* as presented by The Royal Ballet's Touring Company at Covent Garden, 1963

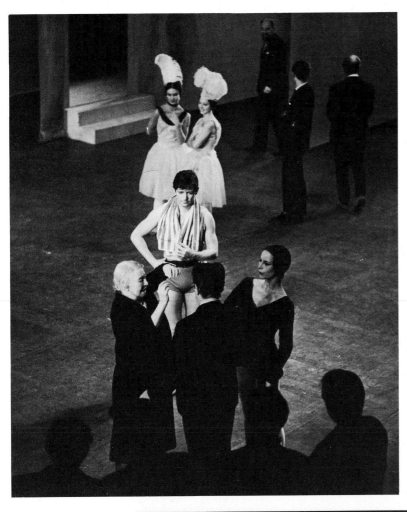

145 In 1964 Sir
Frederick Ashton paid
tribute to Bronislava
Nijinska for her
formative influence on
his creativity by inviting
her to stage *Les Biches*
(and subsequently *Les
Noces*) for The Royal
Ballet. Nijinska is (left)
with Ashton (his back to
the camera) and
Georgina Parkinson
(right) as the Garconne,
with David Blair (facing
them) as the leading
bather, at a stage call.
The revival of these two
Nijinska ballets, so
scrupulously prepared,
reminded a new
audience of her
greatness

146 The wedding scene
from MacMillan's
Romeo and Juliet with
Lynn Seymour and
Christopher Gable as the
young lovers, Gerd
Larsen and Ronald
Hynd in their created
roles as the Nurse and
Friar Laurence, 1965

A variety of guests had continued making impressive appearances with the company. Erik Bruhn appeared with Nadia Nerina to superb effect and also staged for The Royal Ballet a Bournonville divertissement. Yvette Chauviré delighted London yet again with her miraculous *Giselle* and made a sensational debut as Aurora in *The Sleeping Beauty*. Another French dancer, Violette Verdy, on leave from the New York City Ballet, was also a guest. But it was Rudolf Nureyev who became most closely associated with the company; his presence was to stimulate both dancers and audiences and his staging of the Kingdom of Shades scene from *La Bayadère* was a valuable addition to the repertory.

The end of the decade was the end of an era. Kenneth MacMillan had gone to work in Berlin for three years in 1966, but it was announced in the summer of 1970 that he would assume the

147 Yvette Chauviré, première danseuse étoile of the Paris Opéra, appeared in *Giselle*, her most celebrated role, as a guest with The Royal Ballet in 1958

149 Ekaterina Maximova as Masha the heroine of Yury Grigorovich's staging of *The Nutcracker* for the Bolshoy Ballet, as shown at Covent Garden in 1969 – an enchanting performance

148 Margot Fonteyn and Rudolf Nureyev in the final pose of his staging of the Kingdom of Shades scene from *La Bayadère*, 1963. Two years previously the Kirov Ballet had revealed to London the classic beauties of this episode from Petipa's dramatic spectacle. The Royal Ballet dancers eventually achieved such a peak of ensemble excellence in this production that the *Evening Standard*'s annual ballet award was given in 1974 to the corps de ballet

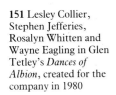

150 Michael Coleman
and Laura Connor in the
closing Butterfly romp
from Jerome Robbins's
hilarious *The Concert*
which entered the
repertory in 1975

151 Lesley Collier,
Stephen Jefferies,
Rosalyn Whitten and
Wayne Eagling in Glen
Tetley's *Dances of
Albion*, created for the
company in 1980

directorship of The Royal Ballet jointly with John Field on the retirement of Sir Frederick Ashton. At the same time Sir David Webster was to leave the Opera House, to be succeeded by John Tooley, and changes were made in the identity of the touring company. Ashton's departure was marked by a Gala which was a loving retrospective glimpse of no fewer than thirty-six of his ballets.

During the summer months Covent Garden was host to American Ballet Theatre and in the autumn the new season began under MacMillan and Field with Lynn Seymour also returning to the company after a period spent in Berlin. Administrative changes took place and John Field resigned from The Royal Ballet to become director of the ballet company at La Scala, Milan. Peter Wright became Associate Director with MacMillan, while continuing his responsibilities with the 'New Group' as the touring company was then called, eventually building it into the Sadler's Wells Royal Ballet of today.

The seven years of MacMillan's directorship were to find him also able to produce a sequence of major ballets which included two full-evening works *Anastasia* in 1971 (a development

152 David Wall as Crown Prince Rudolf and Lynn Seymour as Mary Vetsera in Kenneth MacMillan's *Mayerling*, 1979

153 Lesley Collier as Odette and David Wall as Prince Siegfried with the corps de ballet in Norman Morrice's staging of *Swan Lake*, 1979

154 Natalia Makarova and Anthony Dowell in the second act of *Giselle*, 1972

155 Mikhail Baryshnikov made a series of guest appearances with The Royal Ballet in the late 1970s, culminating in the creation for him of *Rhapsody* by Sir Frederick Ashton to celebrate the eightieth birthday of Queen Elizabeth, The Queen Mother, on 4 August 1980

156 Kenneth MacMillan rehearsing Merle Park and Derek Rencher in the Isadora/Paris Singer pas de deux that follows the announcement of the death of Isadora's children. Kenneth MacMillan's bold two-act treatment of the life of the revolutionary American dancer was first produced by The Royal Ballet in 1981. *Isadora*, with its combination of speech and dance, sought to broaden the horizons of the full-length academic ballet – not least in splitting its leading role between a dancer (Merle Park) and an actress (Mary Miller)

157 Marcia Haydée and
Richard Cragun of
The Stuttgart Ballet as
Katherine and Petruchio
in John Cranko's *The
Taming of the Shrew*. At
the Gala Ballet
Performance given to
celebrate Britain's entry
into Europe on
13 January 1973, Covent
Garden staged a 'Fanfare
for Europe' in which
these two artists danced
a pas de deux that
condensed in
wonderfully funny form
the combative love affair
of Shakespeare's
characters. In 1974 The
Stuttgart Ballet, lately
bereaved of its creator
John Cranko, made its
first appearance at
Covent Garden

158 Peggy Lyman as
Saint Joan in Martha
Graham's *Seraphic
Dialogue* during the first
visit of the Graham
company to Covent
Garden in 1976. The
beautiful designs are by
Isamu Noguchi

159 Lowell Smith,
Virginia Johnson and
members of the corps de
ballet in *The Four
Temperaments* during the
Dance Theatre of
Harlem's first visit to
The Royal Opera House
in 1981

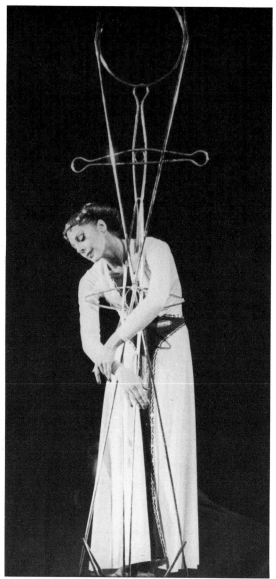

from a one act work he had staged in Berlin), and *Manon* in 1974, both designed to deploy the dramatic as well as the dancing strength of the company which was headed at this time by Sibley and Dowell, Seymour, Park, Mason, Wall and such younger talents as Wayne Eagling, Lesley Collier and Jennifer Penney.

Among works by other choreographers, *Dances at a Gathering* by Jerome Robbins won an immediate place in the affections of the public and was given with a magnificent cast. Other ballets were provided by Hans van Manen, Glen Tetley and John Neumeier, and an especial welcome was given to Sir Frederick Ashton's *A Month in the Country* in 1976. In the following year MacMillan announced his resignation as director of the company in order to devote his time to creativity as the company's principal choreographer, and a direct result of this can be seen in the exceptional achievement of the full evening epic *Mayerling*, first produced in February 1978 with its astounding central role for David Wall as Crown Prince Rudolf and the rich texture of the supporting characters headed by Merle Park as Larisch, Lynn Seymour as Mary Vetsera, Georgina

Parkinson as the Empress Elisabeth and Wendy Ellis as Stephanie.

MacMillan was succeeded as Director of The Royal Ballet by Norman Morrice, at one time Director of the Ballet Rambert, a company whose identity he had helped shape during the 1960s. Under Morrice, the classic stagings were freshly edited and prepared, and important acquisitions came from MacMillan with *La Fin du jour*, *Gloria*, *My Brother, My Sisters* (acquired from Stuttgart) and the controversial full evening *Isadora* for Merle Park and Mary Miller.

During the MacMillan years Rudolf Nureyev continued to make guest appearances and other welcome ex-Kirov visitors were Natalia Makarova, who shone in both the classic and the contemporary repertory, and Mikhail Baryshnikov who made a profound impact in *Swan Lake*, *Romeo and Juliet* and *La Fille mal gardée* and for whom Ashton made *Rhapsody* for the Queen Mother's eightieth birthday celebratory performance. Another birthday at this time was the emotional and joyous evening in which the company saluted Dame Margot Fonteyn's sixtieth birthday in 1979.

160 Merrill Ashley and Sean Lavery of the New York City Ballet in *Square Dance*. These two young dancers epitomised the dazzling skill of the company on its triumphant return to Covent Garden in 1979 after an all-too-long absence of 13 years

The guest companies of the decade were headed by three American troupes. In 1976 Bicentennial Year was celebrated with the first appearance of the Martha Graham Company at Covent Garden (the company was to return in 1979). The storming of the Bastille of classical dance by one of the Earth Mothers of American contemporary dance was a fascinating comment upon the changes wrought in public taste since her first London appearance twenty years before, when she had played to largely uncomprehending audiences. Dance Theatre of Harlem offered yet another and very ebullient aspect of American dance when they appeared at Covent Garden in 1981. The summer of 1979 saw not only the return of Graham but also the first Covent Garden appearance of the National Ballet of Canada and an astounding season by Balanchine's New York City Ballet, who brought a repertory of no fewer than twenty-nine ballets and a company at a pinnacle of magnificence.

A fitting comment upon the essential function of the Opera House as a home for a national ballet is conveyed by events in the summer of 1981 when the Royal Ballet School were seen at their charming best in Ashton's *La Fille mal gardée* and The Royal Ballet gave three 50th anniversary galas on 29 and 30 May. These provided a survey, master-minded by Michael Somes, of something of the growth and achievement of the company. Thirty-five years earlier it had taken up residence at Covent Garden. Now the Royal Opera House was its permanent showcase: a great company had found a great home.

161 The Royal Ballet's three Golden Jubilee Galas in 1981 ended with joyous curtain calls. Dame Ninette de Valois is seen at the very heart of the enterprise she started, with (on her right) Norman Morrice and (on her left), Peter Wright, directors of The Royal Ballet and Sadler's Wells Royal Ballet. Dame Alicia Markova, the company's first ballerina (standing behind Peter Wright), Kenneth MacMillan, principal choreographer of The Royal Ballet (extreme right), and the artists of the two companies representing the entire 50 years' history are applauding Dame Ninette

Opera and Music at Covent Garden

HAROLD ROSENTHAL

To many people the name Covent Garden still means the fruit and vegetable market that for years occupied the area which today has taken on a new look; but to the opera- and ballet-goer, and to the practitioner of those two arts the world over, it means the Royal Opera House – at least ever since 1847 when the second Theatre Royal, Covent Garden, underwent a metamorphosis and became the Royal Italian Opera. However, there had been a theatre on the same site in Bow Street since 1732, and the present building, the third to stand on the site, was the only one built as an opera house; though it became a permanent home for the lyric arts only in 1946 when it re-opened all the year round after the end of the Second World War.

The history of the first two theatres is, for the most part, the history of the great days of the British stage, the days of Garrick and Peg Woffington, the Kembles, Mrs Siddons, Macready and Kean. The first theatre was built by John Rich, who had in his possession 'Letters patent' granted by Charles II to Sir William Davenant, which empowered the holder to build a theatre in the City of London and Westminster. Rich's first theatre had been built in Lincoln's Inn Fields. It was the success of his production there of Gay's *The Beggar's Opera* – 'It made Rich gay and Gay rich' – that enabled him to look for another site on which to build a second theatre. He was able to obtain a lease of a piece of land that was 'contiguous to Bow Street, Hart Street and Covent Garden'. This land belonged to the Duke of Bedford whose forebears had been rewarded with its possession by Henry VIII at the time of the dissolution of the monasteries – Covent Garden having been a *convent* garden, where the monks of Westminster had buried their dead.

On 7 December 1732, Rich was able to open the first Covent Garden Theatre with a performance of Congreve's *The Way of the World*; nine days later its long and important musical life began with a performance of *The Beggar's Opera*. Although Rich's Royal Patent would have allowed him, had he felt so inclined, to use his new theatre exclusively for opera, it was not until just over a century later, in the thirty-ninth year of the life of the second theatre, that Covent Garden became an opera

MR GAY.

162
John Gay (1685-1732), who invented ballad opera with *The Beggar's Opera*: the first production was so popular partly because it dealt with recognisable characters from London's criminal fraternity and partly because of its use of popular tunes

house. There were, however, a number of occasions between 1732 and 1847 when opera was performed at the first two Covent Garden theatres. Artistically, the life of the theatre during that period resembled very closely that of a German Court Theatre, with drama, opera and concerts alternating with each other throughout the season – perhaps in the proportion of two-thirds drama to one-third music.

The first great operatic interlude occurred between 1735 and 1737 after Handel had been forced to withdraw from the King's Theatre in the Haymarket following his quarrel with the famous castrato, Senesino. Handel's company which gave three seasons at Covent Garden included the soprano Cecilia Young, later married to the composer Thomas Arne who wrote most of the ballad operas performed there between 1750 and 1777; the famous tenor, John Beard, who married Rich's daughter in 1759

163 George Frideric Handel (1685-1759): his association with Covent Garden began with a revival of *Il pastor fido* on 9 November 1734 and lasted until shortly before his death

164 Riots in 1763 during a performance of *Artaxerxes* by Thomas Arne (1710-78) – the audience's way of expressing disapproval over increases in seat prices

and later became the proprietor and manager of the house; the sopranos Anna Strada del Po and Maria Negri; and the castrati Giovanni Carestini, Gioacchino Conti Gizziello, who was known professionally by his middle name, and Domenico Annibali. For this remarkable group of singers Handel composed *Ariodante* (1735), *Alcina* (1735), *Atalanta* (1736), *Arminio* (1737), and *Berenice* (1737).

These were not the only works by Handel written for Covent Garden however, for his association with the theatre lasted until 1752, and several of his 'dramatic oratorios' were composed for the annual series of 'Lenten concerts'. These concerts, as their name suggests, were given during Lent when stage performances were forbidden, and they included *Alexander's Feast, Samson, Judas Maccabaeus, Belshazzar, Solomon, Theodora* and *Jephtha*. It is also worth chronicling that the composer's most famous work, *Messiah*, which had received its first performance in Dublin in 1742, had its first performance in England at Covent Garden the following year, and that others of his oratorios, including *Saul* and *Israel in Egypt* were included in the Lenten concerts. But despite the success of all these works with the public Handel lost his complete personal fortune of some £10,000.

165 Carl Maria von Weber (1786-1826) made his first appearance in England at Covent Garden on 9 March 1826 conducting a 'selection' from *Der Freischütz*

If it was Handel whose name dominated the musical scene in the early days of Covent Garden there were also two composers of British birth who contributed to the first hundred years of its musical history, Thomas Arne and Henry Bishop. Arne's *Love in a Village* and *Artaxerxes* both had their premieres at Covent Garden in 1762; the latter was notable not only because Arne himself translated Metastasio's Italian text and set it in Italian style, but because the cast included two famous castrati, Nicolo Peretti and Giusto Ferdinando Tenducci, and the soprano Charlotte Brent, one of Arne's most successful pupils. Because of this expensive cast, seat prices were increased and riots ensued.

In 1808 John Rich's theatre was burned to the ground and the entire contents, including Handel's organ, which he had bequeathed to Rich, were destroyed. A new and grander theatre, designed by Smirke, was built on the same site and opened in 1809. The following year, J.P. Kemble, the manager, engaged as his music director, Henry Bishop.

Bishop is perhaps best remembered today as the composer of 'Home Sweet Home', but he was music director at Covent Garden until 1824. During this period he 'adapted' several foreign operas, including *Don Giovanni*, *Le nozze di Figaro*, *Il barbiere di Siviglia* and *Fidelio* for the theatre, mercilessly re-writing large portions and introducing music of his own into the scores. When criticised for treating Mozart's music in so cavalier a fashion, he replied 'My sole object in so doing was to improve the national taste for opera by rendering English audiences more familiar with truly dramatic music.'

166 Set design by William Grieve for the hall and gallery in Almanzor's Palace, in Act III of Weber's *Oberon*. *The News* for 16 April 1826 reported that although 'this theatre has ever been famous for the spleandour of its scenery...*Oberon* outshines all its predecessors. It is said that near 6,000*l*. has been expended on its production and we can readily believe it.'

In 1824 Bishop had been at Covent Garden for nearly fourteen years, during which time he had been responsible for approximately seventy musical pieces; not unnaturally he asked Kemble for an increase in salary, which was refused. Bishop resigned and in the following month Kemble invited the German composer Carl Maria von Weber to come to Covent Garden, if not officially as Music Director, at least as an honoured guest. Weber was commissioned to compose a work specially for London, the premiere of which he would conduct, as well as four 'oratorio concerts' (these were later increased to five). He would receive a fee of £500 for the opera and £225 for conducting the concerts. The opera was *Oberon*, the composition of which took Weber some two years, and so he did not arrive in London until 1826. Two of his earlier operas, *Der Freischütz* and *Preciosa*, had already been heard at Covent Garden, the former receiving innumerable performances, the latter being given only once.

Weber arrived in London on 5 March 1826 and rehearsals for *Oberon* began four days later; they continued until 11 April, the day before the premiere. During the *Oberon* rehearsal period Weber conducted concerts not only at Covent Garden but also for the Philharmonic Society. Already a very sick man when he arrived in London, Weber managed to conduct the first night of *Oberon*, when the overture was encored and every aria was interrupted two or three times by bursts of applause. In all he conducted twelve performances of *Oberon*, though his health was deteriorating all the time and on 5 June, exactly thirteen weeks after his arrival, he died. His funeral service at St Mary's in Moorfields was attended by many leading musicians, and the entire Covent Garden company took part in the service during which Mozart's *Requiem* was sung. It was to be more than a quarter of a century before another great composer would conduct an opera at Covent Garden; that was in 1853 when Berlioz conducted his *Benvenuto Cellini* which was neither understood nor appreciated and received only one performance.

Before the second Covent Garden Theatre became the Royal Italian Opera in 1847 a number of important operatic events took place there including visits by opera companies from Germany and Belgium, a series of memorable performances by an English company headed by the soprano Adelaide Kemble, and the Covent Garden debut of Maria Malibran. This famous soprano, already a great favourite in London, sang at Covent Garden for the first time on 4 June 1830 when she was heard in the last act of Rossini's *Otello*, opposite the tenor Domenico Donzelli, and in the Countess–Susanna duet from *Figaro* with the soprano Mary Ann Paton.

167 Elizabeth Rainforth (1814-77) and Adelaide Kemble (1814-79) as Adalgisa and Norma in Bellini's *Norma*. Adelaide Kemble was the first British singer to appear as Norma, singing the role in English at Covent Garden in 1841

168 Maria Malibran (1808-36) as Amina in Bellini's *La Sonnambula*, 14 June 1833, a production that she had had transferred from Drury Lane Theatre

169 Playbill for the last night of the German Opera Company's season, 3 July 1833, showing not only a remarkable array of singers but also an amazing selection of operas

170 Sir Michael Costa (1808-84), conductor and Music Director at the Royal Italian Opera 1847-69; in 1867 he was knighted for his services to music

She reappeared in 1833 as a guest artist with a German company which was headed by the legendary Wilhelmine Schröder-Devrient, known as 'The Queen of Tears' and as the soprano who had an enormous influence on Wagner. Schröder-Devrient's Leonore in *Fidelio*, possibly her greatest role, was heard at Covent Garden several times during the summer of 1833, including the last night of the season when the marathon programme also included Act 1 of Weber's *Euryanthe;* and sandwiched between Bethoven and Weber, Act III of Rossini's *Otello* with Schröder-Devrient singing the Moor, and Malibran the part of Desdemona. Then, as an 'extra night' on 12 July, there was heard 'For the first and only time on this stage, the Italian opera, compressed into one act, called *Norma*. The music entirely composed by Bellini'. In this performance, the great Giuditta Pasta, who had created Norma two years earlier in Milan, made her only Covent Garden appearance in the part, with the original Pollione, Donzelli.

Almost exactly a year later the equally famous Giulia Grisi, the tenor Giovanni Battista Rubini, the baritone Antonio Tamburini and the conductor Michael Costa were 'lent' by the King's Theatre in the Haymarket to sing in a performance of *Il barbiere di Siviglia*. It is doubtful whether either Grisi or Costa dreamed on that evening that in little more than a decade Covent Garden would have become their permanent London home and a rival Royal Italian Opera.

The events that led to the second Theatre Royal, Covent Garden, becoming London's second Royal Italian Opera and setting up in rivalry to the long-established Royal Italian Opera in the Haymarket themselves resemble an Italian operatic plot. Under successive managements the King's Theatre in the Haymarket (renamed Her Majesty's on the accession of Queen Victoria), had established itself as one of the most famous lyric theatres in Europe. It had been the scene of the first performances in England of most of the important works by Rossini, Bellini and Donizetti, and had seen the London debuts of all the great Italian singers of the day. Since 1833 the Music Director had been Michael Costa, and in the 1840s the company, which included Giulia Grisi, Fanny Persiani, the tenor Mario, and the baritone Tamburini, was under the management of Benjamin Lumley. This group of artists was known in London operatic circles as *La Vieille Garde*, and in 1839 they declared jointly that none of them would accept an engagement in London unless the rest of their number was also engaged. This led in 1840 to what became known as 'The Tamburini Row'

171 Wagner's *Der fliegende Holländer* was given its first performance at Covent Garden on 16 June 1877, in Italian, as *Il vascello fantasmo*, thirty-four years after its premiere in Dresden

which culminated in a series of nightly demonstrations by the public in the theatre; in the end the management capitulated and re-engaged Tamburini. Two years later Lumley, who had succeeded to the management in 1842, refused to engage the baritone: he quarrelled with Costa, who resigned, and was succeeded by Michael Balfe; and a steady deterioration of musical and artistic standards set in.

By the end of the 1845 season *The Times* wrote about 'Ill-paid and unpaid artists, an interior in disorder, a band and chorus in revolt, shabbiness and poverty rampant within its walls'. By the following summer it had become an open secret in London that Giuseppe Persiani, the husband of the soprano Fanny Persiani and a minor Italian composer had, together with a compatriot, Galletti, purchased the lease of Covent Garden Theatre for £35,000. They were encouraged by Charles Grüneisen, music critic of the *Morning Chronicle* and close friend of Costa who had become the chief propagandist for the establishment of a second Italian Opera House in London. Further financial support came from Frederick Beale, one of the partners of the music publishers,

172 'The overwhelming of the Hall of the Gibichungs' from *Der Ring des Nibelungen*, 1903, conducted by Hans Richter (1843-1916), who conducted his first season at the Royal Italian Opera in 1884, returning in 1903 to conduct his first Covent Garden *Ring*

173 Spy cartoon of Sir Augustus Harris (1852-96) for *Vanity Fair*. Harris was manager at Covent Garden from 1888 to 1896 where he improved musical standards, introducing opera in the original language and doing much to popularise German opera

Cramer, Beale and Company, who was appointed general manager of the new enterprise. The necessary architectural changes to the theatre were made by Benedict Albano, who gained possession of the house in December 1846. By the beginning of April 1847, the new Royal Italian Opera, Covent Garden was ready to open its doors.

At that time it was quite naturally Italian opera that held sway; but it was not only operas by Rossini, Donizetti and Bellini, and later Verdi, that were performed; *all* operas were sung in Italian including Weber's *Der Freischütz* and Mozart's *Die Zauberflöte*, which were given as *Il franco arciero* and *Il flauto magico;* *Les Huguenots* (with which the present Covent Garden opened in 1858) was given as *Gli Ugonotti*, and indeed all the French repertory was sung in Italian, as were all the first Wagner operas to be heard at Covent Garden: *Lohengrin* in 1875, *Tannhäuser* in 1876, and *Der fliegende Holländer*, billed as *Il vascello fantasmo*, in 1877. It was not until 1892 that the word Italian was dropped from the Theatre's title, and it became the Royal Opera House. This was during the regime of Augustus Harris who raised the musical and artistic standards of

the theatre to heights not hitherto achieved. Operas were then generally given in their original language and Wagner really came into his own with Covent Garden's first *Ring* cycles conducted by Gustav Mahler in 1892.

Wagner's popularity increased during the 1890s and the first decade of this century, mostly due to the efforts of the famous Bayreuth conductor Hans Richter who was brave enough to persuade Covent Garden to embark on giving the *Ring* in English in 1908 and 1909. Richter, in association with his British assistant Percy Pitt, had hoped that this would lead to the establishment of a permanent English national opera. The scheme was thwarted by the implacable attitude of the Grand Opera Syndicate who held the purse strings at Covent Garden. Far more to the syndicate's liking were the starry evenings with Dame Nellie Melba and Enrico Caruso, Luisa Tetrazzini and John McCormack; and there was no denying the appeal of the then new kind of Italian opera, called *verismo*, whose leading exponents were Puccini, Leoncavallo, Mascagni and Giordano. French operas like *Louise* and *Samson et Dalila* were also proving popular.

174 Peter Cornelius (1865-1934) as Siegfried and Minnie Saltzmann-Stevens (1874-1950) as Brünnhilde in Act III of *Siegfried*. Cornelius was chosen by Richter to sing Siegfried in the English *Ring* performances of 1908 and 1909 and Saltzmann-Stevens made her Covent Garden debut singing Brünnhilde in the 1909 cycle

Since the time when opera was first performed there, Covent Garden has played host to the majority of the greatest singers in the world of opera from the days of the castrati until today. Of course all singers who have appeared on its stage have not been stars; and there have been far more singers whose names have long since vanished than great artists whose names have become part of operatic history.

Sopranos and tenors have always seemed to be more glamorous than contraltos and basses – baritones have always had a rather special appeal of their own – and since Covent Garden became an opera house each decade has been dominated by a soprano, tenor and baritone.

The dominating figures in the 1850s were Giulia Grisi, Mario and Tamburini. Grisi sang in London every season from 1834 until 1861, first at Her Majesty's Theatre, and then from 1847 at Covent Garden; she had created the role of Adalgisa in *Norma* (though later she also became a famous Norma) and was the first Elvira in *I Puritani* and Norina in *Don Pasquale*. Théophile Gautier wrote of her: 'Where can one find another head as if moulded by Phidias such as she carries so proudly and nobly on her marble-like shoulders? ...As for her voice it is unique; tender in love passages, grand in anger and indignation, and in sorrow melting the hearts of those who hear her. Under her spell what was only an opera becomes a tragedy and a poem.'

Her regular partner on stage, and from 1844 in private life, was the tenor Mario. Originally Giovanni Matteo, Cavaliere di Candia, he first sang in London in 1839, and at Covent Garden in 1847, where he appeared every season until 1867, returning to make his farewell in 1871. He was the first London Ernesto in *Don Pasquale*, Duke of Mantua, John of Leyden (*Le Prophète*), and Roméo; his voice was generally considered to have been one of the most beautiful ever heard, and he sang with elegance and style; handsome in appearance and with acting abilities unusual for a singer at that time, he became the idol of Victorian opera goers. The baritone who most often partnered Grisi and Mario was Tamburini who created many roles in operas by Bellini and Donizetti, and sang in several first performances in London.

175 Marietta Alboni (1823-94) as Arsace, Giulia Grisi (1811-69) as Semiramide and Antonio Tamburini (1800-76) as Assur in Rossini's *Semiramide*, which opened the Royal Italian Opera House on 6 April 1847. Grisi's costume shows the influence of contemporary fashion

176 Madame Anese, Jean-Baptiste Faure (1830-1914), Adelina Patti and Giovanni Mario (1810-83) Gounod's *Faust*, in 1864. *Faust* was one of the most popular operas of the late nineteenth century and was performed at Covent Garden every season from 1863 to 1911

After Grisi came the even more famous Adelina Patti who made her Covent Garden debut in 1861 as Amina in *La Sonnambula* at the age of eighteen. Soon after, she sang Zerlina in the *Don Giovanni* performance in which Grisi was singing her last Donna Anna – Grisi, the retiring diva, and Patti, the new star, thus made their only appearance together on any stage. Patti sang in twenty-five consecutive seasons at Covent Garden, where she appeared in some thirty different roles; she was London's first Aida and Juliette (Gounod), and became the most highly paid singer of her day – 200 guineas a performance and 5000 dollars in America. She had a clause in her contract excusing her from attending rehearsals and another stipulating the size in which her name was to appear on posters.

Frederick Gye, who was Covent Garden's Manager from 1849 to 1877, mounted several operas specially written for Patti by long-forgotten and undistinguished composers. In most of these she was partnered by the French-born tenor, Ernest Nicolini whom she married in 1886. The favourite baritone of the Patti era was also French, Jean-Baptiste Faure; he made his Covent Garden debut in 1860 and continued to sing there until the mid-1870s. He was much admired as Don Giovanni, Hamlet (Ambroise Thomas) and William Tell.

177 Dame Nellie Melba (1861-1931) as Juliette in Gounod's *Roméo et Juliette*, which she first sang at Covent Garden in 1889, marking the start of her great London triumphs

177A Melba as Violetta in Verdi's *La traviata*, one of her most famous roles

178 & 179 Jean de Reszke (1850-1925) as Lohengrin and his brother Edouard (1853-1917) as Heinrich I in Wagner's *Lohengrin* which they first sang together at Covent Garden in 1888

180 Enrico Caruso (1873-1921) as Canio in Leoncavallo's *Pagliacci*: he first sang the role at Covent Garden on 19 May 1904

The Canadian soprano, Emma Albani who, like Patti, made her Covent Garden debut as Amina, arrived in London in 1872. At first her repertory overlapped that of Patti, but Gye, whose son married Albani, managed to keep the peace between his two prima donnas by giving Albani the Wagner roles – Senta, Elisabeth and Elsa, as well as Mignon, the *Figaro* Countess and Margherita in Boito's *Mefistofele*, all parts that were not in Patti's repertory. But Patti's true successor at Covent Garden was the Australian soprano, Nellie Melba.

The reign of Melba began in 1888, the year in which Augustus Harris took over the theatre, and continued virtually without a break (she missed only one season) until 1914; she returned in 1919, made guest appearances in the house with the British National Opera Company, and gave her farewell performance in 1926. At first she was a high coloratura soprano, famous for her Rosina, Lucia, Gilda and Violetta; later she sang such lyric roles as Marguerite, Desdemona and Mimì, and she even appeared as the *Siegfried* Brünnhilde, her one great failure. Her acting abilities were somewhat restricted, and many found her interpretations cold. But she was indeed the *prima donna assoluta*, having the final word in the engagements of singers and the castings of the operas in which she appeared.

181 The audience settling into the Stalls for a Prom performance. The first twentieth century Prom was given in 1971 since when Prom seasons have become an annual event

THE PROMENADE CONCERTS, COVENT GARDEN.

182 The stage during a Promenade Concert organised by W. Freeman Thomas (1844-98)

She also had the unmusical distinction of having a dessert and a kind of toast named after her.

Melba's favourite partners were the elegant Polish tenor, Jean de Reszke (he had a brand of cigarettes named after him), and the one and only Enrico Caruso. De Reszke sang at Covent Garden every year except one from 1888 until 1900, and Caruso for seven of the seasons between 1902 and 1914. De Reszke was Melba's regular Roméo and Caruso her Rodolfo; though of course both sang many other roles at Covent Garden. There were two baritones who were great favourites during the reign of Melba; the French Victor Maurel, who was Verdi's first Iago and Falstaff, both of which roles he sang at Covent Garden, and the Italian, Antonio Scotti, who was also a fine Iago and Falstaff, and was London's first Scarpia and Sharpless.

Over the last few years, 'Covent Garden Proms' have come to mean fully–staged performances of opera and ballet, and sometimes recitals by international celebrities, before an audience which includes a large proportion of young people. The Stalls area is cleared of seating and seven hundred promenade places are sold at low prices for people to sit on the floor. But Covent Garden had already held promenade concerts in the

183 Caricatures of Louis Antoine Jullien (1812- 60), the French showman-conductor who initiated the annual Promenade Concerts at Covent Garden in the 1840s

184 & 185 'A Picturesque and Entertaining Adjunct to the London Telegraph System', 1899, an early attempt to reach a wider audience by the live relay of performances

186 Sir Thomas Beecham (1879-1961) was instrumental in introducing the operas of Richard Strauss to English audiences – despite the reservations of the censor

Gerontius with John Coates, Louise Kirkby Lunn and the Hallé Orchestra; and in 1909 and 1910 Richter and Artur Nikisch conducted a series of Sunday evening concerts with the London Symphony Orchestra. Thomas Beecham conducted his own orchestra in several concerts during his first Covent Garden season in 1910; and when he was Artistic Director of the Opera House in the 1930s, his regular Sunday afternoon Beecham Concerts, with the London Philharmonic, included such distinguished soloists as Richard Tauber, Claudio Arrau, Bronislaw Hubermann and Ida Haendel. And it was, appropriately enough, at Covent Garden that Fyodor Chaliapin made his last appearance in England in a recital in February 1937.

Such events remained, however, interludes in the musical life of the theatre, which continued to be primarily a home for opera, even though the seasons were relatively short compared with those of the 1970s and 1980s. And whereas, in the nineteenth century, it had been the great singers whose personalities had helped shape the nature of those seasons, in the twentieth century it was the turn of first the conductor, and later the producer, to dictate the style of the operatic productions.

Just as the names of Mahler at the Vienna Opera and Toscanini at La Scala were synonymous with those theatres' great days earlier this century, so the name of Thomas Beecham has become linked with Covent Garden in the period 1910 to 1913, 1919 to 1920, and especially 1932 to 1939. When Beecham gave his first opera season at Covent Garden he was only thirty; he had formed the New Symphony Orchestra in 1906, re-named it the Beecham Symphony Orchestra in 1909, the year he had become reconciled with his father with whom he had quarrelled. His father, the wealthy Sir Joseph Beecham whose fortune had been made from the famous Beecham Pills ('worth a guinea a box'), was ready to indulge his son's passion for opera. As Beecham wrote in his autobiography: 'My recent experience with *The Wreckers* [he had staged Ethel Smyth's opera at His Majesty's Theatre for six matinee performances in June 1909] had strongly revived in me an interest that had lain dormant for seven years, although during that time I had been reflecting continuously upon the many-sided problems of operatic representation, not solely from the musical angle...I had begotten a desire to try my hand at a venture under the conditions where the various ideas and theories I had been forming could take living shape. But this sort of thing was unrealizable without powerful backing, which up to the moment had not been forthcoming'.

nineteenth century, which began in the 1840s with those conducted by Louis Antoine Jullien – those were just two of his more than thirty Christian names. He possessed all the showman's tricks, including being handed a jewelled baton on a silver salver and wearing white gloves whenever he conducted Beethoven, whose Fifth Symphony he decorated with the addition of side-drums, a saxophone and four ophicleides!

Jullien's Proms continued until 1856 and then, when the present theatre opened, he was succeeded by Alfred Mellon, whose concerts, known as the Mellon Proms, continued until 1867. Mellon himself was the Music Director of two English opera companies that gave winter seasons at Covent Garden in the 1850s and 1860s: the Pyne-Harrison Company and the Royal English Opera Company Limited.

In 1867 there was a series of concerts conducted by Johann Strauss; and it was at a Promenade Concert in September 1893 that Saint-Saëns's *Samson et Dalila*, which the censor would not allow to be produced on stage because of its religious content, was first heard in England.

In 1904 Hans Richter conducted an Elgar Festival at Covent Garden which included the first performance in London of *The Dream of*

THE OPERA THAT WILL "ELEKTRIFY" LONDON.
TO SING THE MOST ARDUOUS SCORE EVER WRITTEN: CHARACTERS IN STRAUSS'S "ELEKTRA,"
TO BE PRODUCED FOR THE FIRST TIME AT COVENT GARDEN ON SATURDAY.

SWEET HARMONIES OF MODERN MUSIC.

187 Anna von
Mildenburg (1872-1947)
as Clytemnestra, with
(insets) Hermann
Weidemann (1871-1919)
as Orestes and Edyth
Walker (1867-1950) as
Elektra in the British
premiere of *Elektra* at
the Royal Opera House
in 1910. *The Sketch*
reported the score as
being 'the most difficult
ever written...both for
the singers and the
orchestra'

188 'The orchestra
during a typical opera
performance of the
future?' Although
Beecham championed
the operas of Richard
Strauss during his first
seasons at Covent
Garden, not everyone
shared his taste for
'modern music'.
Cartoon from the
Daily Mirror,
19 February 1910

By the end of 1909, however, Beecham senior
had provided the wherewithal that enabled his
son to launch an experimental season at Covent
Garden to open in February 1910. The Grand
Opera Syndicate, who regarded young Thomas
as something of an upstart and amateur, looked
rather askance when their own Music Director,
Percy Pitt, accepted an invitation from Beecham
to assist him during his first season and to
conduct three of the operas in the repertory:
Humperdinck's *Hänsel und Gretel*, Debussy's
L'Enfant prodigue and Sullivan's *Ivanhoe*. In
addition, Beecham invited the young Bruno
Walter to come to London to conduct
The Wreckers and *Tristan und Isolde*, while
Beecham himself conducted Delius's *A Village
Romeo and Juliet* and the first performances in
England of Richard Strauss's *Elektra* (Strauss
himself conducted two of the nine performances
at a fee of £200 a night).

In his introduction to the propectus for the
season Beecham stressed the fact that: 'In
modern opera the conductor and the orchestra
play as important a part as the singer, and in this
as in other departments, including staging, etc.,
the management has acted on the same principle
as in the selection of the casts'. It is no wonder
that Melba and her like reacted unfavourably
when they returned to Covent Garden in 1919
and found Beecham firmly installed there. But
that is jumping ahead in the story of Beecham at
Covent Garden.

Just as Strauss's *Elektra* occupied most of the
rehearsal time for Beecham's first Covent
Garden season so did the same composer's

Plate 33 John Braham (1774-1856) as Orlando in *The Cabinet*, 9 February 1802, for which role the tenor composed all his own music

Plate 34 Giulia Grisi (1811-69) and her husband Giovanni Mario (1810-83) as Lucrezia and her son Gennaro in the first Covent Garden production of Donizetti's *Lucrezia Borgia*, 15 May 1847

Plate 35 Adelina Patti (1843-1919) as Zerlina in Mozart's *Don Giovanni*, 1892

Plate 36 Joan Sutherland in the title role of Donizetti's *Lucia di Lammermoor*, 1959, the production that launched her international career and marked Franco Zeffirelli's debut as a producer at Covent Garden

Plate 37 A new production of Verdi's *Aida*, 28 October 1957, conducted by Rafael Kubelik, produced by Margherita Walmann, and designed by Salvatore Fiume, with David Kelly as the High Priest, Amy Shuard as Aida, Fedora Barbieri as Amneris and Joseph Rouleau as The King

Plate 38 Verdi's *Don Carlos*, the production chosen to commemorate the centenary of the opening of the present theatre, May 1958, conducted by Carlo Maria Giulini, produced and designed by Luchino Visconti. The cast included Gré Brouwenstijn, Jon Vickers, Tito Gobbi and Boris Christoff

Plate 39 The coronation scene from Moussorgsky's *Boris Godunov* with Boris Christoff in the title role, 1958. Christoff gave his first stage performance as Boris at Covent Garden in 1949

Plate 40 Maria Callas (1923-77) in the title role of Puccini's *Tosca*, 21 January 1964, a production that combined her vocal and acting abilities to outstanding effect

Plate 41 Hildegard Hillebrecht as the Empress and James King as the Emperor in *Die Frau ohne Schatten*, 14 June 1967, by Richard Strauss, conducted by Georg Solti, produced by Rudolf Hartmann, with sets designed by Josef Svoboda and costumes by Carl Toms

Plate 42 Forbes Robinson as Moses and Richard Lewis as Aaron in the British premiere of Schoenberg's opera, 28 June 1965, conducted by Georg Solti, produced by Peter Hall and designed by John Bury

Plate 43 Geraint Evans as Dulcamara in the first post-war production of Donizetti's *L'elisir d'amore* by The Royal Opera, 18 December 1975, conducted by John Pritchard, produced by John Copley and designed by Beni Montresor

Plate 44 Berlioz's *Les Troyens*, with Josephine Veasey as Dido, 17 September 1969, conducted by Colin Davis, produced by Minos Volanakis and designed by Nicholas Georgiadis

Plate 45 The final scene from Saint-Saëns's *Samson et Dalila*, 28 September 1981, with Jonathan Summers as the High Priest, and Shirley Verrett and Jon Vickers in the title roles. Conducted by Colin Davis, produced by Elijah Moshinsky, designed by Sidney Nolan and with choreography by David Bintley

Plate 46 Placido Domingo in the title role of Offenbach's *Les Contes d'Hoffman*, 15 December 1980, with Agnes Baltsa as Giulietta and Claire Powell as Nicklauss, conducted by Georges Prêtre, produced by John Schlesinger, with sets designed by William Dudley and costumes by Maria Björnson

Plate 47 Stuart Burrows as Ferrando, Kiri te Kanawa as Fiordiligi, Agnes Baltsa as Dorabella and Thomas Allen as Guglielmo in a revival of *Così fan tutte*, 1981, conducted by Colin Davis, produced by John Copley, with sets designed by Henry Bardon and costumes by David Walker

Plate 48 Verdi's *Luisa Miller*, 19 June 1978, with Katia Ricciarelli in the title role and Luciano Pavarotti as Rodolfo in a new production conducted by Lorin Maazel, produced and designed by Filippo Sanjust

Salome in his second, and *Der Rosenkavalier* in his third. These Beecham seasons were given in either the winter or autumn, for the pattern of the 'Grand International' seasons in which Verdi, Puccini, and Wagner held sway could not be altered – and the Syndicate was certainly not going to invite this young British conductor to participate in the 'Grand' season. Because of exclusive rights granted by Ricordi to the Grand Opera Syndicate, Beecham was unable to include any of the more popular Italian and French works in his repertory: he did, however, unearth some rarities, including Thomas's *Hamlet*, D'Albert's *Tiefland*, and *Les Contes d'Hoffmann* (never previously given at Covent Garden), as well as the more frequently performed *Le nozze di Figaro* and *Don Giovanni*. But except for *Salome*, audiences were small and the critical reactions on the whole harsh. 'Something was wrong somewhere' wrote Beecham, 'and I am not at all sure where the fault lay, with the public or myself'.

Beecham ran into trouble with the Lord Chamberlain over *Salome* and *Der Rosenkavalier;* in the first opera because of its biblical subject, which meant that changes had to be made in the libretto before it was considered suitable for the British stage; in the second, because objections were made to both the bed and Baron Ochs's reference to it in the last act of the opera. Beecham was told that either the bed could be seen and the offending words removed, or that Ochs could sing the words, but that the bed should remain hidden. Beecham decided on the second course, and alway referred to this action as 'a nearly perfect example of our British love of compromise'.

By the time Beecham returned to Covent Garden in 1919 he had formed the famous Beecham Opera Company which prospered during the 1914-1918 war and helped launch the careers of several British singers. He refused to bow to public outcry against German music, and continued to include Wagner operas in his repertory; and his productions of Mozart's operas, especially *Figaro* staged by Nigel Playfair, set a standard.

Towards the end of the war Beecham and his father became involved in the purchase of the whole Covent Garden estate at the cost of some two million pounds; the area covered included not only the market but also the Theatre Royal, Drury Lane and the Royal Opera House. The intricacies of Beecham's finances are too complicated to discuss here; but the fact that in 1919 Beecham found himself in possession of the Opera House was, to quote Sir Thomas, 'More honourable than profitable'.

The redoubtable Grand Opera Syndicate invited Beecham to join their Board and to collaborate with them in putting on an international season in the summer of 1919 – nothing German or Austrian of course, but a predominantly Italian and French repertory. Grandiose plans were announced including the first Covent Garden *Simon Boccanegra* and the engagement of Toscanini – neither materialised;

189 Elisabeth Schumann (1885-1952) as Sophie and Delia Reinhardt (1892-1974) as Octavian in a new production of *Der Rosenkavalier*, 1924, conducted by Bruno Walter (1876-1962)

190 Lauritz Melchior (1890-1973) as Tristan and Frida Leider (1888-1975) as Isolde. They were considered the finest Tristan and Isolde of the inter-war years

nor did a production of Puccini's *Trittico* which Toscanini was to have conducted and which had to wait until the following year for its presentation at Covent Garden, but without Toscanini.

The 1919 and 1920 Beecham seasons were not successful financially nor, on the whole, artistically. By 1919 Beecham's loss from his operatic enterprises had reached £104,000, but this was only a fraction of his total liabilities which were listed as £2,131,571 – his assets being £74,724. By the end of the 1920 summer season at Covent Garden in which the Diaghilev Ballets Russes was also participating, a bankruptcy order was made against Beecham, and at the same time his own Beecham Opera Company went into voluntary liquidation. It was to be another twelve years before Beecham conducted again at Covent Garden.

Before the return of Beecham in 1932 the guiding light of the Covent Garden season was Bruno Walter; indeed the years 1924 to 1931 were very much a golden age of German opera including as they did the famous series of *Der Rosenkavalier* performances with the incomparable cast of Lotte Lehmann, Delia Reinhardt, Elisabeth Schumann and Richard Mayr; *Der Ring des Nibelungen, Die Meistersinger von Nürnberg*, and *Tristan und Isolde* with Frida Leider, Lehmann, Maria Olczewska, Lauritz Melchior, Friedrich Schorr, Rudolf Bockelmann, Herbert Janssen, Ivar Andrésen and Alexander Kipnis; and a legendary *Don Giovanni* with Leider, Lehmann, Schumann and Mariano Stabile. Italian opera fared less well, though there were, of course, the performances of *Turandot* in which Eva Turner, who had established her reputation in Italy in the mid-1920s, was welcomed home and recognised as one of the great sopranos of the day – she also sang Aida and Santuzza with great success. And one should not forget the three seasons between 1929 and 1932, when the American-born Rosa Ponselle triumphed as Norma and Violetta; Beniamino Gigli as Andrea Chénier, the Duke of Mantua, and in Puccini; and Stabile as Falstaff, Iago and Scarpia.

191 Rosa Ponselle (1897-1981) as Norma. Bellini's opera was specially revived for her Covent Garden debut on 28 May 1929

192 Beniamino Gigli (1890-1957) as Andrea Chénier in Giordano's opera of that name. He chose to make his debut at every major opera house in this role

193 Eva Turner as Turandot, the role in which she established her international reputation. She first sang Turandot at Covent Garden on 5 June 1928 and on the occasion of her last performance on 28 February 1948

By the end of the 1931 season London's operatic future was in the melting pot. Colonel Eustace Blois, the Managing Director of the Grand Opera Syndicate which was backed financially by the naturalised Hungarian financier, F.A. Szarvasy, had managed to keep opera going since 1928; but the seasons were short – a mere eight or nine weeks – and for the rest of the year the Opera House, other than the occasional short season of opera in English and a little ballet, was turned into a *palais de danse*. The socialist government of Ramsay MacDonald had granted the first subsidy to opera in the country's history – £25,000 a year to be paid through the BBC: a fraction of its licence income. But by the autumn of 1931 the world recession was having disastrous effects. The autumn season of opera in English brought only 25% capacity houses, and the Board announced the cancellation of the 1932 summer season. There was an outcry in the press, and it was decided to bring Beecham back into the Covent Garden fold to put on a four-week Wagner Festival. This meant the dropping of the faithful Bruno Walter and getting the agreement of several foreign singers to accept much reduced fees.

The lease of the theatre was due to expire at the end of the 1933 season, and Beecham was already looking ahead far beyond that date. It soon became obvious that unless Beecham was virtually in sole control, difficulties would arise – and even when he was in command, his arbitrary way with finance often brought him close to disaster. None the less he had rich and powerful friends in society and in the City, none more so than Lady Cunard, who drummed up support.

Between 1934 and 1939 Beecham and his new board took steps to modernize the theatre; those steps included a new block of offices and dressing rooms, a chorus rehearsal room behind the stage area, the installation of a new lighting system and a cyclorama. Beecham, with the help of Geoffrey Toye, brother of the music critic Francis Toye, and manager of the Sadler's Wells Opera, broadened the repertory. He harboured ideas of becoming a kind of overlord of all London opera, introducing works like *Arabella*, *Schwanda the Bagpiper*, *La Cenerentola*, *L'Italiana in Algeri* (both the latter with the gifted and attractive Conchita Supervia). A German producer, Otto Erhardt, one of the many refugees from Nazi Germany, was engaged.

Wilhelm Furtwängler, Hans Knappertsbusch, Fritz Reiner and Felix Weingartner came to conduct the German repertory; Gino Marinuzzi and Vittorio Gui the Italian performances. Giacomo Lauri-Volpi, Giovanni Martinelli and Beniamino Gigli strengthened the cast of the 1936-39 Italian seasons; Kirsten Flagstad made her Covent Garden debut in 1936; and Richard Tauber delighted audiences in Mozart in 1938 and 1939. There were Sunday concerts, evening recitals, autumn and winter seasons, and a short but memorable visit in November 1936 by the Dresden State Opera when Strauss himself conducted a performance of his *Ariadne auf Naxos*, during which the German Ambassador, Ribbentrop, shocked a large section of the audience by giving the Nazi salute from the Royal Box.

By the last week of the 1939 June season, with war a little more than two months away, patrons found a preliminary prospectus for 1940 tucked

194 Conchita Supervia
(1895-1936) made her
Covent Garden debut as
Angelina in Rossini's
La Cenerentola in June
1934

into their nightly programmes. 'It is Sir
Thomas's hope to place the summer season on a
more permanent basis than hitherto, and to
establish a regular company of the most
distinguished artists, with a wider and more
progressive policy'. A list of twenty-five operas
was announced from which the season's
repertory would be chosen; it included Gluck's
Iphigénie en Tauride, Berlioz's *Les Troyens*,
Puccini's *La fanciulla del West*, and
Mussorgsky's *Boris Godunov*; all of which found
their way into the Covent Garden operatic
repertory after the war, but not, alas, under
Beecham, who except for his appearances in
1951 with *The Bohemian Girl* and
Die Meistersinger von Nürnberg, never conducted
opera again at Covent Garden.

During the war years, no opera was staged at
Covent Garden and the theatre became once
more a *palais de danse*. Mecca Cafés Ltd leased
the building from Covent Garden Properties
Ltd and it was the latter's chairman, Philip Hill,
who was instrumental in rescuing the theatre at
the end of the war. Hill first approached Harold
Holt, the impresario, and offered him the
chance of taking the lease of the theatre. Holt,
feeling unable to shoulder the full responsibility
of running the opera house himself, asked Hill if
he could pass on the offer to the music
publishers, Boosey and Hawkes – both Leslie
Boosey and Ralph Hawkes being directors of
Holt's concert agency. Hill and his colleagues
offered no objections to this proposal, and
Boosey and Hawkes agreed to examine the
position. They took the lease of the building as
from 1 January 1945 and the theatre was able to
re-open on 20 February 1946 with a production
of *The Sleeping Beauty*. The Royal Opera House
now had resident opera and ballet companies
and they both participated in a production of
Purcell's *The Fairy Queen* in December 1946,
and the Covent Garden Opera Company gave its
first performance in January 1947, in *Carmen*.

195 'In preparation for
the opening of the
Grand Opera Season at
Covent Garden:
Sir Thomas Beecham in
conference with
Dr Otto Erhardt, one of
the producers, at a
Lohengrin "dress
parade" ', *Illustrated
London News*, 20 April
1935

196 Elisabeth Schwarzkopf as Violetta in Verdi's *La traviata*, with Paolo Silveri as Giorgio Germont, Kenneth Neate as Alfredo Germont and Marion Nowakowski as the Baron Douphol in a new production, 6 April 1948, conducted by Reginald Goodall, produced by Tyrone Guthrie and with scenery and costumes designed by Sophie Fedorovitch

197 Members of the Vienna State Opera Company on stage with Sir David Webster during the Company's visit to Covent Garden in 1947. Artists included Elisabeth Schwarzkopf, Ludwig Weber, Erich Kunz, Paul Schöffler, Ljuba Welitsch, Sena Jurinac and Hans Hotter

198 Edith Coates as Carmen and Kenneth Neate as Don José in the Covent Garden Opera Company's first production of Bizet's *Carmen* in January 1947, conducted by Karl Rankl and designed by Edward Burra

199 Renata Tebaldi and Ramon Vinay in a performance of Verdi's *Otello* conducted by Victor de Sabata, during La Scala's first visit to the Royal Opera House in September 1950

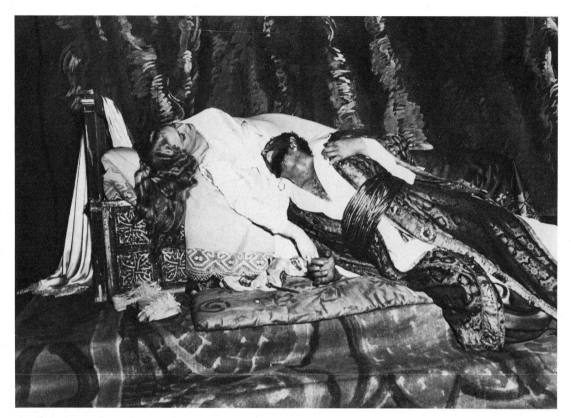

200 Joan Sutherland as Jenifer and Richard Lewis as Mark, with Michael Langdon and Edith Coates as The Ancients, in the World Premiere of *The Midsummer Marriage*, 1955, Michael Tippett's first opera for the Royal Opera House, conducted by John Pritchard, produced by Christopher West, designed by Barbara Hepworth and with choreography by John Cranko

201 David Webster (1903-71), was Covent Garden's General Administrator from 1945 to 1970. Following the Second World War, he successfully established the Royal Opera House as the permanent home of Sadler's Wells Ballet and the Covent Garden Opera Company; both received their Royal Charters during his regime

When in 1892 the Royal Italian Opera, Covent Garden, had become the Royal Opera, the name referred to the building and not the company that performed there – indeed there was no permanent Covent Garden company at that time; but when, in October 1968, Her Majesty Queen Elizabeth II approved the recommendation of the then Home Secretary, James Callaghan, that the Covent Garden Opera should become The Royal Opera, it was the Company and not the building that housed it that was being honoured. Up to 1939 it can be truly said that Covent Garden's operatic history had been made up of brilliant operatic memories; there had been no sense of continuity, and only two or three vain attempts to establish a permanent operatic tradition. So in 1945, the newly-formed Covent Garden Opera had had to start from scratch.

To expect a native operatic tradition to emerge in ten, fifteen or even twenty years was expecting too much – yet many did expect exactly that; and so the infant company was attacked on all sides by critics, both professional and amateur. What is amazing is that within twenty-five years The Royal Opera emerged as one of the leading operatic organizations in the world; and although England did not achieve in that short period what Germany and Italy had in

some three hundred or so years, the standards of The Royal Opera are respected by singers and conductors all over the world. That this happened was due in the first place to David Webster and the three Music Directors who worked with him: Karl Rankl (1946-51), who put in the spade work and built up the opera company from nothing – and who received more knocks than thanks for his efforts; Rafael Kubelik (1955-58) who believed in ensemble and was able to put on Berlioz's *Trojans* with only one guest artist; and Georg Solti (1961-71) whose aim was simply to make Covent Garden the best opera house in the world, and who brought excitment and glamour to the theatre. During the two periods when the Opera Company lacked a Music Director, it was largely due to David Webster's patience and good common sense, and to the help of Lord Harewood, that the company nurtured such fine singers as Joan Sutherland, Jon Vickers, Geraint Evans and the late Amy Shuard. Then there were the regular guest conductors, Erich Kleiber, Rudolf Kempe, Otto Klemperer, Carlo Maria Giulini and John Pritchard, all of whom helped develop the confidence of British artists and the reputation of Covent Garden.

202 Karl Rankl (1898-1968), Covent Garden's first post-war Music Director, introducing Erich Kleiber (1890-1956) to the Royal Opera House Orchestra

204 Georg Solti made his Covent Garden debut in 1959 conducting performances of Richard Strauss's *Der Rosenkavalier*, and became Music Director in 1961

203 Rafael Kubelik was Music Director at Covent Garden from 1955 to 1958. His successes included the English stage premiere of Janáček's *Jenůfa* in 1956 and he returned to conduct this opera in 1970

205 Colin Davis made his Covent Garden debut in 1960 conducting *La Valse* and *Le Baiser de la fée* for The Royal Ballet. His debut with the Opera Company followed in 1965 with *Le nozze di Figaro* and in September 1971 he succeeded Georg Solti as Music Director

206 John Tooley, who succeeded David Webster as General Administrator in 1970, is here seen escorting Her Majesty the Queen and Her Majesty the Queen Mother at the Royal Opera House

The growth has continued in the John Tooley-Colin Davis years; these have seen the emergence of a new generation of British and Commonwealth singers including Kiri te Kanawa, Thomas Allen, Gwynne Howell, Robert Lloyd, Yvonne Kenny, and Robert Tear to mention just a few; the engagement of several distinguished guest conductors, including Claudio Abbado, Carlos Kleiber, Charles Mackerras, Zubin Mehta and Riccardo Muti; the memorable performances of Mozart, Berlioz, Wagner and Tippett; the creation of a new image and the attempts to broaden the audiences, especially with the Proms. Perhaps one can level the criticism that The Royal Opera is no longer a Company as it was in the 1960s, but then, as Colin Davis has himself said, there is only one great international opera company – the one that appears in all the world's leading opera houses today. None the less, the Colin Davis years have allowed us to hear most of the world's leading singers and conductors; and even if we were disappointed when Peter Hall's collaboration with Covent Garden came to an abrupt end in 1971, there have been some memorable productions since then, including the Götz Friedrich *Ring* and *Lulu*, and several works staged by Elijah Moshinsky and John Copley.

Everyone will have his or her outstanding memories of the last quarter of a century at Covent Garden; and I, like most other opera fans, have often re-lived some of those great evenings: Kirsten Flagstad and Hans Hotter in Wagner; Maria Callas in whatever role she sang;

the Giulini-Visconti *Don Carlos* of 1958 with Gré Brouwenstijn, Fedora Barbieri, Jon Vickers, Tito Gobbi and Boris Christoff; the Solti-Peter Hall *Moses and Aaron;* Klemperer's *Fidelio* with Sena Jurinac as Leonore; the impact of *The Trojans;* Janet Baker, especially as Vitellia in *La clemenza di Tito* conducted by Colin Davis; Ileana Cotrubas and Geraint Evans in *Don Pasquale* and *L'elisir d'amore;* and the recent revivals of *Die Meistersinger von Nürnberg* and *Tristan und Isolde* both conducted by Colin Davis with casts that certainly at this time are not equalled at Bayreuth.

Contemporary Covent Garden audiences have also had the opportunity of hearing outstanding singers not only in operatic performances, but also in recital. A recent feature of the Covent Garden season has been the series of International Celebrity Recitals given on Sunday evenings by such distinguished artists as Janet Baker, Teresa Berganza, Montserrat Caballé, Elisabeth Schwarzkopf, Dietrich Fischer-Dieskau, Carlo Bergonzi, Nicolai Gedda, and many others; far less frequently there have been orchestral concerts when the Opera House's orchestra has emerged from the anonymity of the pit to take its place on stage in full view of the public. But concerts and recitals are by no means a recent Covent Garden innovation.

207 Peter Pears as von Aschenbach in Benjamin Britten's *Death in Venice* which was given its first London performance at the Royal Opera House by the English Opera Group in 1973, conducted by Steuart Bedford, produced by Colin Graham, with sets designed by John Piper and costumes by Charles Knode

208 Eric Garrett as Antonio, Victor Braun as Count Almaviva, Geraint Evans as Figaro, Reri Grist as Susanna and Kiri te Kanawa as Countess Almaviva in Mozart's *Le nozze di Figaro*, 1971. It was her performances as the Countess that brought Kiri te Kanawa her first international acclaim

209 José Carreras as Werther and Frederica von Stade as Charlotte in Massenet's *Werther* 1980, a co-production with English National Opera

210 Kirsten Flagstad as Brünnhilde and Hans Hotter as Wotan in *Die Walküre*, 1948. Their performances after the War did much to re-establish the popularity of Wagner's works

211 Maria Callas as Norma, the role in which she made her Covent Garden debut on 8 November 1952

212 Otto Klemperer with members of the cast of Beethoven's *Fidelio* which he conducted and produced in 1961; Sena Jurinac as Leonore, Jon Vickers as Florestan, John Dobson as Jaquino and Elsie Morison as Marzelline

213 Janet Baker as
Alceste, with Robert
Tear as Admète, in
Gluck's *Alceste*, the role
in which she gave her
Covent Garden farewell
opera performance on
15 December 1981

In the immediate post-war period there were
recitals by Mischa Elman, Moura Lympany,
Jennie Tourel, and concerts by the Vienna
Philharmonic and other visiting orchestras. In
May 1952, Erich Kleiber, who did so much for
Covent Garden in the early 1950s, conducted a
performance of Beethoven's Choral Symphony
with Sylvia Fisher, Constance Shacklock, Edgar
Evans and Norman Walker as soloists, as a first
step towards founding a welfare fund for chorus
and orchestra to assist them in times of need. It
was Kleiber who helped to give British singers
and musicians their self-respect and so lay those
foundations on which Kempe, Giulini, Kubelik,
Solti and Davis have so successfully built.

In the days of the prima donna, the conductor
counted for little, and it was only in the German
repertory that there was any real discipline. All
that began to change when Beecham arrived at
Covent Garden in 1910; it continued in the
inter-war years, first with Bruno Walter, then
Beecham again, Furtwängler and Vittorio Gui.
Producers have by contrast been something of a
post-war phenomenon; rarely if ever before
1939 was the name of a producer even
mentioned in the programme at Covent Garden
or indeed in any other opera house – there were
a few exceptions like Carl Ebert, first in Berlin
and then at Glyndebourne, and Max Reinhardt
at Salzburg; but by and large it was the stage
manager who told the singers where to stand

and what to do. All that has changed and
distinguished men of the theatre have entered
the world of opera; and if at times their work
has sparked off controversy, so much the better.
From the British theatre have come Peter
Brook, Peter Hall, Tyrone Guthrie, John
Gielgud; from Italy Luchino Visconti and
Franco Zeffirelli; and from Germany, Götz
Friedrich. It has been the visual side of opera
that has divided audiences in recent years; and
audience reaction to much that is seen on the
operatic stage, not only at Covent Garden, but
elsewhere in Europe and America, has become
an accepted – if unacceptable – part of the ritual
of opera going.

In the world of opera there have always been
claques, official and unofficial, and singers and
conductors have often been the victims of
hostile demonstrations from sections of the
audience. Audience 'participation', long
established in Italy, has recently spread to opera
houses all over the world. It is difficult to
understand just what pleasure the booers get
from giving voice to their feelings; I suppose the
argument is that if one can cheer a good
performance, then one is at liberty to hiss or boo
a bad one – surely complete silence would be
better?

214 Ljuba Welitsch as
Salome and Franz
Lechleitner as Herod in
the controversial Peter
Brook production of the
Richard Strauss *Salome*,
1949, conducted by Karl
Rankl and designed by
Salvador Dali

215 Carlo Bergonzi as
Manrico and Martina
Arroyo as Leonora in
Verdi's *Il trovatore*,
1978. The first
performance of this
production, conducted
by Carlo Maria Giulini,
produced by Luchino
Visconti and designed
by Filippo Sanjust was
given in 1964

216 Tito Gobbi as
Scarpia in Franco
Zeffirelli's memorable
production of Puccini's
Tosca in 1964,
conducted by Carlo
Felice Cillario with sets
by Renzo Mongiardino
and costumes by Marcel
Escoffier

217 Gwyneth Jones as Brünnhilde, Bengt Rundgren as Hagen, Jean Cox as Siegfried, Jerker Arvidson as Gunther and Helena Döse as Gutrune in *Götterdämmerung*, 1978

218 *Das Rheingold*, 1978, the entry of the Gods into Valhalla: Robert Lloyd (Fasolt), Donald McIntyre (Wotan), Hermann Becht (Donner), Josephine Veasey (Fricka), Rachel Yakar (Freia) and Robert Tear (Froh). The 1978 revival of Götz Friedrich's production of *Der Ring des Nibelungen* conducted by Colin Davis included the first Prom performances of a complete cycle

219 Birgit Nilsson as Brünnhilde in Hans Hotter's production of Wagner's *Der Ring des Nibelungen*, 1962-1964, conducted by Georg Solti and designed by Günther Schneider-Siemssen

220 Piero Cappuccilli as Boccanegra and Mirella Freni as Amelia in Verdi's *Simon Boccanegra*, conducted by Claudio Abbado, produced by Giorgio Strehler and designed by Ezio Frigerio, during La Scala's exchange visit with The Royal Opera in 1976

221 Karan Armstrong as Lulu and Günter Reich as Dr Schön in the British Premiere of the three-act version of Alban Berg's *Lulu* (Act III realised by Friedrich Cerha), 16 February 1981, conducted by Colin Davis and produced by Götz Friedrich, and with designs by Timothy O'Brien

Covent Garden opera audiences can be as cruel as their counterparts in Italy and Germany, but they can also be the warmest; and they are faithful to their long-established favourites. Perhaps there is no such thing as a typical Covent Garden opera audience: Verdi and Puccini attract quite a different kind of public from that which comes to worship at the Wagnerian shrine; and an audience for Sutherland or Caballé, which will include its fair share of what have been called 'canary-fanciers', is not the same audience that comes to hear Jon Vickers as Peter Grimes or a performance of *Wozzeck* or *Lulu*. Since Covent Garden re-opened its doors in 1946, it has staged over one hundred different operas – one hundred and twenty if one includes those novelties given by visiting companies from abroad like Strauss's *Capriccio*, *Die Liebe der Danäe*, Rossini's *La Cenerentola* and Blomdahl's *Aniara*. And that means that Covent Garden has afforded London opera audiences the opportunity of becoming one of the best-informed in the world.

222 Placido Domingo first sang Verdi's *Otello* at Covent Garden on 5 February 1980, with Carlos Kleiber conducting

223 Montserrat Caballé as Leonora in Verdi's *Il trovatore*, 1975, conducted by Anton Guadagno, in the Luchino Visconti production rehearsed by Charles Hamilton, and designed by Filippo Sanjust

224 Ileana Cotrubas as Antonia in Offenbach's *Les Contes d'Hoffmann*, 15 December 1980, in a new production conducted by Georges Prêtre, produced by John Schlesinger, with costumes designed by Maria Björnson and sets by William Dudley. This production was the first to be recorded at the Royal Opera House by Covent Garden Video Productions Ltd, in association with the BBC, for worldwide television distribution

225 Verdi's *Macbeth*, 1981, with Renato Bruson in the title role and Renata Scotto as Lady Macbeth, conducted by Riccardo Muti, produced by Elijah Moshinsky and designed by John Napier

Contributors

Andrew Saint was born in Shrewsbury and educated at Christ's Hospital and Balliol College, Oxford. He taught at the University of Essex for three years and has been Architectural Editor to the *Survey of London* at the Greater London Council since 1974. His biography of the Victorian architect Norman Shaw appeared in 1976, and a study by him of the architectural profession will be published in 1983.

B.A. Young was born in London and educated at Highgate School. After working at the Amalgamated Press, and a spell as a freelance writer, he was commissioned into the Lancashire Fusiliers and served in Africa, Italy and Germany. After being demobilised, he joined the staff of *Punch*, on which he worked for a number of years, before joining the *Financial Times* in 1964: he was Editor of that paper's Arts Page for seven years, and still writes for it in addition to other freelance work.

Mary Clarke is the Editor of *The Dancing Times*, dance critic for *The Guardian* and a contributor to *Encyclopedia Brittanica*. She was London correspondent of New York's *Dance Magazine* from 1943 to 1955, and London Editor of *Dance News* of New York from 1953 to 1970. She was assistant editor to Arnold Haskell on *The Ballet Annual*, and with David Vaughan edited *The Encyclopedia of Dance and Ballet*; her books include *The Sadler's Wells Ballet, A History and an Appreciation*, and *Dancers of Mercury, the Story of Ballet Rambert*, in addition to seven books on ballet on which she has collaborated with Clement Crisp.

Clement Crisp is ballet critic of *The Financial Times*, London correspondent of *Les Saisons de la Danse*, Librarian and tutor at the Royal Academy of Dancing, and tutor in dance history at the Laban Centre, Goldsmith's College. He is the author of a dozen books on dancing, seven of them in collaboration with Mary Clarke.

Harold Rosenthal was born in London and educated at the City of London School and the University of London. After Army service he took up a teaching career. With Lord Harewood he launched the magazine *Opera*, of which he was assistant editor from 1950 to 1953, since when he has been its Editor. Between 1950 and 1956 he was Archivist of the Royal Opera House. He is a contributor to numerous international musical publications, and a frequent lecturer and broadcaster. His publications include two books about Covent Garden and a recently published autobiography, *My Mad World of Opera*.

Acknowledgements

On behalf of the Royal Opera House, the editors wish to thank all those who have helped make this book possible.

We firstly wish to thank Commercial Union Assurance who have sponsored its publication, and Bunzl Pulp and Paper (Sales) Limited who have kindly donated the paper: the generosity of both has made publication possible at a time of financial stringency.

We should like to thank our contributors for their patience throughout the production of the book and for their assistance in the selection of pictures and the provision of captions: the final selection, and the wording of all captions has, however, been our own responsibility.

We are deeply grateful to our colleagues at the Opera House, especially Ken Davison, Janet Judd and Katharine Wilkinson for their advice and assistance; and to Janet Jempson and Rosemary Runciman for their tireless help.

Our designers, Logos Design, and our printers, Jolly and Barber have supported us nobly through a tight schedule.

Philip de Bay and Ken Jackson of Image Photography gave speedy and skillful assistance with photography and we also wish to thank Lise Agate and Helen Ottaway for additional picture research; and Douglas Matthews for his index. Among the many people who have helped us to find pictures we particularly wish to thank the staff of the Theatre Museum at the Victoria and Albert Museum, and Raymond Mander and Joe Mitchenson.

More specifically we wish to thank the copyright owners listed below for their permission to reproduce the illustrations indicated: we have not been able to trace every copyright owner and would be glad to hear from anyone who has not been contacted.

For any errors which remain we, of course, take responsibility.

Francesca Franchi and Henry Fryer

Audrain Press Agency, no 100; Clive Barda, plates 6, 43, 45, 46, nos 205, 222, 224 and page 6; Baron (courtesy of BBC Hulton Picture Library), no 127; Baron (courtesy of Mr Gwyer Gibbs), no 198; British Architectural Library/RIBA, no 36; B.B.C., no 134; British Library Newspaper Library, no 123; British Museum, nos 11, 30, 62; British Travel and Holidays Association, plate 36; Christina Burton, no 5; Clarke – Crisp Collection, nos 110, 112, 116; Country Life, nos 40, 41, 43, 51; Courtauld Institute of Art, no 37; Anthony Crickmay, nos 146, 150, 151, 152, 155, 223; Daily Herald, no 58; Frederika Davis, nos 144, 149; Zoë Dominic, plates 47, 48, nos 141, 148, 154, 161, 201, 213, 219; Robert Eddison Collection, no 12; Mary Evans Picture Library, no 13; John Garner, no 207; Garrick Club, plate 8, nos 81, 82; GLC, nos 15, 16, 19, 35; GMW Partnership, no 17; Guildhall Library, nos 2, 33; Hood, Hughes and York, no 46; Illustrated London News Picture Library, nos 48, 172, 177, 194; Kemsley Picture Service, no 3; Keystone Press Agency, nos 42, 52; Richard Leacroft, nos 7, 18, 38; Serge Lido, nos 130, 135; Raymond Mander and Joe Mitchenson Theatre Collection, plate 7, nos 32, 39, 45, 66, 69, 83, 88, 91, 97, 103, 162, 182, 184, 185; Edward Mandinian, nos 129 (courtesy of the Theatre Museum, Victoria and Albert Museum), 197; H.J. Mydtskov, no 138; National Film Archive, nos 105, 106; National Monuments Record, nos 31, 126; National Portrait Gallery, nos 72, 74, 86, 89, 163; Walter Owen, no 131; E. Piccagliani, no 220; Press Association, no 181; Publiofoto, no 199; Stuart Robinson, no 218; Houston Rogers (courtesy of the Theatre Museum, Victoria and Albert Museum), plates 23, 32, 37, 38, 39, 40, 44, nos 145, 147; Harold Rosenthal, no 192; Royal Opera House Archives, plates 1, 2, 5, 10, 17, 18, 19, 33, 34, nos 1, 6, 8, 9, 10, 14, 21, 22, 24, 25, 26, 27, 34, 57, 59, 61, 65, 67, 70, 73, 79, 80, 84, 89, 92, 93, 94, 96, 98, 107, 108, 109, 113, 114, 115, 118, 119, 120, 125, 164, 165, 167, 168, 169, 170, 171, 173, 174, 176, 177A, 178, 179, 180, 183, 186, 187, 188, 189, 190, 191, 193, 196; Lady Sachs, no 49; Frank Sharmann, plate 20; Snowdon, no 132; Donald Southern, nos 153, 206, 215; Leslie E. Spatt, plate 24, nos 142, 156, 157; Sport and General Press Agency, no 212; Martha Swope, no 158; Theatre Museum, Victoria and Albert Museum, plates 3, 4, 9, 11, 12, 13, 14, 15, 35, nos 4, 23, 28, 29, 60, 63, 64, 68, 71, 75, 76, 78, 85, 87, 95, 99, 102, 111, 117, 121, 122, 175, 195; The Times, no 101; Eileen Tweedy, plate 8, nos 81, 82; Underwood Commercial Studios, no 124; University of London Library (Sterling Library), plate 16, no 166; University of Warwick, History of Art Department, no 77; Jack Vartoogran, no 159; G.B.L. Wilson, no. 143; Reg Wilson, plates 21, 22, 25, 26, 27, 28, 29, 30, 31, 41, 42, nos 20, 50, 54, 160, 204, 208, 209, 217, 221, 225; Roger Wood, nos 128, 136, 137, 210, 211, 214

Cover and jacket illustration
Watercolour by E.M. Barry of the Royal Italian Opera House as seen from Bow Street. This picture was drawn before the theatre was completed and shows statues on the roof and a frieze on the tympanum which were not included in the finished building. The painting was presented to the Governors of the Grand Opera Syndicate by Lucas Brothers, builders of the present theatre.
Property of the Royal Opera House.

Index

Note: All references, including those to captions of black and white pictures, are to page numbers only, except for references to captions of colour plates, which are indicated thus: pl.1 etc.

Abbado, Claudio, 113, 119
Adam, Adolph, 64
Adams, David, pl.31
Aitken, Christine, pl.30
Albani, Emma, 100
Albano, Benedetto (or Benedict), 21-3, 31, 97
Albert, François Decombe, 64
Alboni, Marietta, 98
Allen, Thomas, pl.47; 113
Alonso, Alicia, 75, 76
American Ballet Theatre (*formerly* Ballet Theatre), 75, 76, 77, 86
Amiconi, Jacopo, 14, 42
Anderson, J.H., 22, 67
Anderton, Elizabeth, 80
Andrésen, Ivar, 106
Andreyanova, Yelena, 64
Anti-Corn Law League, 21, 56-7
Armstrong, Karan, 119
Arne, Thomas, 91, 92, 93
Arrau, Claudio, 103
Arroyo, Martina, 117
Arts Council of Great Britain, 36
Arvidson, Jerker, 118
Ashbridge, Bryan, 78
Ashmole, David, pl.24, 30
Ashton, Sir Frederick, pl.21, 23, 25, 26; 70, 75-6, 81, 82, 83, 86, 87, 89-90
audience reaction, 116, 119
Austin, 64
Australian Ballet, 81
Azuma Kabuki Dancers and Musicians, 78

Babil and Bijou (spectacle), pl. 18; 66
Bailey, James, 39
Baker, Dame Janet, 113, 116
Balanchine, George, 69, 72, 75, 78, 79, 82, 90
Balfe, Michael, 96
Ballet Russe de Monte Carlo, 70-73, 77
Ballets des Champs Elysées, 75
Ballets Russes (Russian Ballet), 67, 69-71, 106
bals masqués, 67, 68
Baltsa, Agnes, pl.46, 47
Barbieri, Fedora, pl.37; 113
Bardon, Henry, pl.47
Baronova, Irina, 72-3
Barrez, Jean Baptiste, 64
Barry, Ann, 45
Barry, Sir Charles, 27
Barry, Edward Middleton, pl.5; 27-35, 37
Barry, Spranger, 45
Baryshnikov, Mikhail, 87, 89
Beale, Frederick, 56, 96
Beard, John, 15, 46, 91
Beaton, Cecil, pl.21
Becht, Hermann, 118
Bedford, Dukes of (and Estate), 12, 14, 26, 28, 42, 91

Bedford, 4th Earl of, 12
Bedford, Steuart, 114
Beecham Opera Company, 105-6
Beecham, Sir Joseph, 67, 103-5
Beecham, Sir Thomas, 35, 67, 69, 103-8, 116
Beggar's Opera, The, see Gay, John
Benois, Alexandre, 66
Berganza, Teresa, 113
Bergonzi, Carlo, 113, 117
Beriosova, Svetlana, 75, 78, 81
Berlioz, Hector, 94
Bernasconi, Francis, 19
Betterton, Thomas, 43
Betty, Master (William Henry West), 48-9
Beverley, William Roxby, 28, 32, 34
Bishop, Sir Henry, 93-4
Björnson, Maria, pl.46; 121
Blair, David, pl.23; 78, 81, 83
Blois, Col. Eustace, 107
Blum, René, 72
Bockelmann, Rudolf, 106
Bolm, Adolf, 67, 71
Bolshoy Ballet (Moscow), 79, 81, 84
Boosey and Hawkes (company), 36, 108
Boosey, Leslie, 108
Booth, Barton, 43
Boucicault, Dion, 55, 66
Boulton and Watt (Birmingham), 19
Bournonville, August, 78, 80, 84
Bradwell, 54
Braham, John, pl.33
Brandt, F., 35
Braun, Victor, 114
Brent, Charlotte, 93
British Broadcasting Corporation, 107, 121
British Fire Prevention Committee, 35
British National Opera Company, 100
Britten, Benjamin, 76
Brook, Peter, 116, 117
Brouwenstein, Gré, pl.38; 113
Bruhn, Erik, 78, 80, 84
Bruson, Renato, 121
Bryson, Bill, 38
Buckle, Richard, 78
Bunn, Alfred, 53, 56
Burra, Edward, 109
Burrows, Stuart, pl.47
Bury, John, pl.42
Byre, Oscar, 64
Byron, George Gordon, Lord, 54
Bystander, The (journal), 73

Caballé, Montserrat, 113, 119, 120
Callaghan, James, 111
Callas, Maria, pl.40; 113, 115
Camargo Society, 70
Cappuccilli, Piero, 119
Carreras, José, 114
Caruso, Enrico, 40, 97, 100, 101
Casati, Giovanna, 64
castrati, 91, 92
Catalani, Angelica, 51
censorship, 43, 55
Cerha, Friedrich, 119
Cerrito, Fanny, 66
Chabannes, Marquis de, 19
Chaliapin, Fyodor, 103
Channon, Paul, 38
Charles II, King, 11, 41, 91
Charles, Prince of Wales, 38
Chatfield, Philip, 78
Chauviré, Yvette, 75, 78, 84
Christoff, Boris, pl.38, 39; 113
Cibber, Susannah Mary, 45

Cibber, Theophilus, 42
Cillario, Carlo Felice, 117
circuses, 56, 61
Clive, Kitty, 44
Coates, Edith, 109
Coates, John, 103
Cockerell, C.R., 31
Coleman, Michael, pl.26; 85
Collier, Lesley, 85, 86, 89
Colman, George, the elder, 15, 46-7
Commonwealth Festival (1965),81
Congreve, William: *The Way of the World*, 14, 42, 91
Connor, Laura, pl.26; 85
Cooke, George Frederick, 48
Copland, Alexander, 19
Copley, John, pl.43, 47; 113
Cornelius, Peter, 98
Coronation Gala (1911), 67, 69; (1953), 40
Costa, Sir Michael, 21, 95-6
Cotrubas, Ileana, 113, 121
Covent Garden Market, 35, 36
Covent Garden Opera Trust, 36
Covent Garden Properties Ltd (*later* English Property
    Corporation), 36, 108
Covent Garden Video Productions Ltd, 121
Cox, Jean, 118
Cramer, Beale and Co, 21, 56, 96
Cranko, John, pl.30; 76, 80, 88, 110
Cumberland, Richard, 45
Cunard, Maud Alice, Lady (Emerald), 107

Dali, Salvador, 76, 77, 117
Dance Theatre of Harlem, 88, 90
Danilova, Alexandra, 69, 72, 73, 75, 77
Dauberval, Jean Bercher, 63, 64
Davenant, Sir William, 11, 41, 43, 91
Davis, Sir Colin, pl.44, 45, 47; 112, 113, 116, 118, 119
de Basil, Colonel W., 71-3, 75
Defries, Jonas & Son, 32
de Reszke, Edouard, 100
de Reszke, Jean, 100, 101
Derman, Vergie, pl.29
Desplaces, Henri, 64, 66
Destinn, Emmy, 40
de Valois, Dame Ninette, pl.28; 70, 73, 81, 90
Diaghilev, Sergey, pl.32; 66-7, 69-71, 106
Dibdin, Thomas, 49
Dobson, John, 115
Dolin, Anton, 69-70, 73, 75, 77
Domingo, Placido, pl.46; 120
Donzelli, Domenico, 94-5
d'Or, Henriette, 66
Döse, Helena, 118
Dowell, Anthony, pl.31; 81, 87, 89
Doyle, Desmond, 78, 82
Dresden State Opera, 107
Drury Lane Theatre, pl.12; 11-12, 15, 20, 35, 41, 43, 47,
    50, 63
Dubrovska, Felia, 69
Dudley, William, pl.46; 121

Eagling, Wayne, pl.21; 85, 89
Ebert, Carl, 116
Edward VII, King, 31
Edwards, Leslie, 81
Eglevsky, André, 75, 77
electricity: installed, 32, 34-5
Elizabeth II, Queen, 40, 111, 113
Elizabeth, Queen Mother, 87, 89, 113
Ellis, Wendy, 89
Elman, Mischa, 69, 116
Elssler, Fanny, 64, 65
Elvin, Harold, 75

Elvin, Violetta, 75, 78
English National Opera, 114
English Opera Group, 114
English Property Corporation *see* Covent Garden
    Properties Ltd
Erhardt, Otto, 107, 108
Escoffier, Marcel, 117
Espinosa, Léon, 66
Evans, Edgar, 116
Evans, Sir Geraint, pl.43; 111, 113, 114

Fabbri, Flora, 64
Faucit, Helen, 53, 54
'Fanfare for Europe' (1973), 88
Faure, Jean-Baptiste, 99
Fayer, Yury, 79
Fedorovitch, Sophie, 109
Ferri, Domenico, 22
Field, John, 81, 86
Fielding, Henry, 43
Fifield, Elaine, 78
Fille mal gardée, La (ballet), pl.23; 63, 64, 81, 90
films, 56, 62
fires: 1808, 15, 50, 93; 1856, 22-3, 26, 67, 68; 1956, 33-4
Fischer-Dieskau, Dietrich, 113
Fisher, Sylvia, 116
Fitzpatrick, Thaddeus, 46
Fiume, Salvatore, pl.37
Flagstad, Kirsten, 107, 113, 115
Flaxman, John, 16, 28
Flindt, Flemming, 80
Floral Hall, pl.7; 24, 26-8, 33-4
Fokine, Mikhail, 75
Fonteyn, Dame Margot, pl.20, 21, 32; 75, 78, 79, 80-81,
    84, 89
Fox and Henderson (contractors), 27
Fracci, Carla, 80
Franklin, Frederic, 75, 77
Free Trade Bazaar, pl.4
Freni, Mirella, 119
Friedrich, Götz, 113, 116, 118, 119
Frigerio, Ezio, 119
Fuoco, Sophie, 64
Furtwängler, Wilhelm, 107, 116

Gable, Christopher, 80-1, 82, 83
Galletti, 56, 96
Galster, Amalia, 64
Garrett, Eric, 114
Garrick Club, 54
Garrick, David, 44-6, 48, 91
gas-lighting, 19-20, 32, 34
Gautier, Théophile, 98
Gay, John: *The Beggar's Opera*, 12, 41-2, 54, 91
Gedda, Nicolai, 113
George III, King, 45
George V, King, 67
Georgiadis, Nicholas, pl.44
German Opera Company, 95
Gielgud, Sir John, 116
Gigli, Beniamino, 106-7
Gilpin, John, 80
Giulini, Carlo Maria, pl.38; 111, 113, 116, 117
GMW Partnership, 36
Gobbi, Tito, pl.38; 113, 117
Goldsmith, Oliver, 46
Goodall, Reginald, 109
Goodman's Fields Theatre, 12, 43-4
Graham, Colin, 114
Graham, Martha (and Dance Company), 88, 90
Grahn, Lucile, 64
Grand Ballet de Monte Carlo (*later* du Marquis de Cuevas),
    75, 77
'Grand International' seasons, 105

Grand Opera Syndicate, 34-5, 97, 104-5, 107
Grant, Alexander, 78, 79, 81
Green, Jane, 46
Grey, Beryl, 75, 76, 78
Grieve family (scene painters), pl.4, 16; 20, 64, 93
Grigoriev, Serge, pl.32; 71, 75
Grigorovich, Yury, 81, 84
Grimaldi, Joseph, pl.9; 49-50, 60
Grisi, Giulia, pl.34; 95-6, 98-9
Grissell, Henry, 27, 30-1, 33
Grist, Reri, 114
Grüneisen, Charles, 96
Guadagno, Anton, 120
Guest, Ivor, 64
Gui, Vittorio, 107, 116
Guthrie, Sir Tyrone, 109, 116
Gye, Ernest, 33
Gye, Frederick: rescues Covent Garden 22; reconstruction,
    23, 26-8, 31-3; portrait, 26; statue, 29; death, 33; and
    dance, 66; and fire, 67; and Patti, 99-100

Haendel, Ida, 103
Hall, Sir Peter, pl.42; 113, 116
Hamilton, Charles, 120
Hammerstein, Oscar, 67
Handel, Georg Frideric, pl.1; 14, 50, 91-3
Hansen, Joseph, 66
Harewood, George Henry Hubert Lascelles, 7th Earl of,
    111
Harris, Sir Augustus, 33-4, 97, 100
Harris, Thomas, 15, 20, 47, 52
Hart, John, 81
Hartmann, Rudolf, pl.41
Harvey, Sir John Martin, 56, 62
Hawkes, Ralph, 108
Haymarket Opera House, 12-13, 15; see also Her Majesty's
    Theatre; King's Theatre; Queen's Theatre
Hazlitt, William, 51
heating, 19
Helpmann, Robert, pl.20, 25, 28; 75
Hempel, Frieda, 40
Hepworth, Barbara, 110
Her Majesty's Theatre, Haymarket, 64, 96
Highwood, June, pl.30; 82
Hill, Philip, 108
Hillebrecht, Hildegard, pl.41
Hippisley, Elizabeth, 45
Hogarth, William, 41-2
Holden, Stanley, 81
Holland, Henry, 13, 15, 19-20
Holt, Harold, 108
Horton, Priscilla, 54
Hosking, Julian, pl.21
Hotter, Hans, 109, 113, 115
Howell, Gwynne, 113
Hubermann, Bronislaw, 103
Hynd, Ronald, 83

ice-skating, 74
Imperial Russian Ballet, 67
International Celebrity Recitals, 113

Jackson, George, and Sons, 31
Jackson, Rowena, 78
Janssen, Herbert, 106
Jefferies, Stephen, 85
Johnson, Samuel, 46
Johnston, Mrs H., pl.14
Jones, Gwyneth, 118
Jones, Inigo, 12
Jullien, Louis Antoine, 67, 68, 102, 103
Jurinac, Sena, 109, 113, 115

Kanawa, Kiri te, pl.47; 113, 114

Karsavina, Tamara, 67, 70, 71
Kean, Charles, 52
Kean, Edmund, pl.10; 51-2, 91
Keats, John, 51
Kelly, David, pl.37
Kelly, Desmond, 82
Kelly, Michael, 50
Kemble, Adelaide, 51, 94
Kemble, Charles, 20, 49, 51-2, 55
Kemble, Fanny, 51, 52
Kemble, John Philip, pl.11, 13; 15, 20, 48, 49, 50-1, 52,
    93-4
Kemble, Roger, 47
Kemble, Stephen, 49
Kempe, Rudolf, 111, 116
Kenny, Yvonne, 113
Kent, William, 12
Keynes, John Maynard, Baron, 75
Kidd, Michael, 76
Killigrew, Thomas, 11
King, James, pl.41
King's Theatre, Haymarket, 63, 91, 96
Kipnis, Alexander, 106
Kirov Ballet, Leningrad, 79-81, 84
Kleiber, Carlos, 113, 120
Kleiber, Erich, 111, 112, 116
Klemperer, Otto, 111, 113, 115
Knappertsbusch, Hans, 107
Knode, Charles, 114
Knowles, Sheridan, 52-4
Kshessinskaya, Mathilde F., 66-7
Kubelik, Rafael, pl.37; 111, 112, 116
Kunz, Erich, 109
Kyasht, Gyorgy, 67
Kyasht, Lydia, 67

Lambert, Constant, 75-6, 79
Lancaster, Sir Osbert, pl.23; 82
Lander, Harald, 79
Langdon, Michael, 110
Lapauri, Alexander, 81
Laporte, Pierre, 64
Larsen, Gerd, pl.29; 83
Larsen, Niels Bjørn, 78
La Scala, Milan, 110, 119
Last, Brenda, 80
Lauri-Volpi, Giacomo, 107
Lavrovsky, Leonid, 79, 81
Lechleitner, Franz, 117
Lecomte, Madame, 64
Lehmann, Lotte, 106
Leider, Frida, 105, 106
Lennon, Dennis, 39
Lenten concerts, 92
Leroux, Pauline, 64
Lewis, Richard, pl.42; 110
Lichine, David, 72-3, 75-6
Lifar, Serge, 69-70, 72, 75, 78
Lincoln's Inn Fields Theatre, 11-13, 41-3, 91
Lloyd, Robert, 113, 118
Londesborough, William Henry Forester Denison,
    Baron (later 1st Earl of), 66
London Transport Museum, 33
Lopokova, Lydia, 70
Lord Chamberlain, 43-4
Lucas, Charles and Thomas (Lowestoft builders), 27-8, 33
Lumley, Benjamin, 96
Lunn, Louise Kirkby, 103
Lympany, Moura, 116
Lytton, Edward George Earle Lytton Bulwer-, 1st Baron:
    The Lady of Lyons, 53

Maazel, Lorin, pl.48
McCormack, John, 97

Macdonald, Nesta, 69
MacDonald, Ramsay, 107
McIntyre, Donald, 118
Mackerras, Charles, 113
Macklin, Charles, 44-8
MacLeary, Donald, 81
MacMillan, Kenneth, pl.22, 27, 31; 76, 80-1, 82, 83, 84,
    86, 87, 89, 90
Macready, William Charles, 20, 52-5, 91
Mahler, Gustav, 97, 103
Makarova, Natalia, 79, 87, 89
Malibran, Maria, 94, 95
Manen, Hans van, 89
Manners, Lady Diana (Cooper), 62
Marinuzzi, Gino, 107
Mario (Giovanni Matteo, Cavaliere di Candia), pl.34; 96,
    98, 99
Markevitch, Igor, 70
Markova, Dame Alicia, 69-70, 75, 77, 90
Martinelli, Giovanni, 107
Mary, Queen of George V, 67
Mason, Monica, pl.27; 81, 89
Massine, Léonide, 69, 70, 72, 73, 75-6, 77
Mathews, C.J., 20, 54-5
Maurel, Victor, 101
Maximova, Ekaterina, 81, 84
May, Pamela, 75
Mayr, Richard, 106
Mazurier, Monsieur, 63
Mecca Cafés Ltd., 36, 73, 108
Mehta, Zubin, 113
Melba, Dame Nellie, 40, 97, 99, 100-1, 104
Melchior, Lauritz, 105, 106
Mellon, Alfred, 103
Messel, Oliver, 39, 40, 73
Metropolitan Ballet, 75
Mildenburg, Anna von, 104
Miller, Mary, 87, 89
Mongiardino, Renzo, 117
Monti, Rafaelle, 28, 31
Montresor, Beni, pl.43
Moreton, Lee see Boucicault, Dion
Morison, Elsie, 115
Morrice, Norman, 86, 89, 90
Morse, David, pl.30
Moshinsky, Elijah, pl.45; 113, 121
Mudie, Miss (child actress), 49
Muti, Riccardo, 113, 121

Napier, John, 121
National Ballet of Canada, 90
Neate, Kenneth, 109
Negri, Maria, 92
Nerina, Nadia, pl.23; 78, 81, 84
Neumeier, John, 89
New Symphony Orchestra, 103
Newton, Christopher, pl.29
New York City Ballet, 77-8, 80, 81, 89, 90
Nicolini, Ernest, 99
Nijinska, Bronislava, pl.29; 71, 76, 83
Nijinsky, Vaslav, 67, 69, 70
Nikisch, Artur, 103
Noguchi, Isamu, 88
Nolan, Sir Sidney, pl.27; 45
Nouveau Ballet de Monte Carlo, 75
Novikov, Laurent, 71
Novosielski, Michael, 15
Nowakowski, Marion, 109
Nureyev, Rudolf, pl.21; 80-1, 84, 89

O'Brien, Timothy, 119
O'Connell, Daniel, 56, 57
Olczewska, Maria, 106
Old Price riots, pl.11; 20, 50-1

Original Ballet Russe, 75
Orlov, Nicholas, 75
Osbaldiston, 53

Pagava, Ethery, 77
pantomimes, 12, 41, 42, 43, 49, 50, 54, 56, 58-60, 63
Paris Opéra Ballet, 66, 78, 79,
Park, Merle, pl.26; 81, 87, 89
Parkinson, Georgina, 83, 89
Pasta, Giuditta, 95
patents (theatre), 11, 20, 41, 46, 91
Paton, Mary Ann, 94
Patti, Adelina, pl.35; 29, 99-100
Pavarotti, Luciano, pl.48
Pavlova, Anna, 67, 71
Pears, Peter, 114
Penney, Jennifer, pl.21, 26; 89
Perrot, Jules, 66
Persiani, Fanny, 21, 96
Persiani, Giuseppe, 21, 56, 96
Petit, Roland, 75
Pigmalion (Sallé), 63
Phelps, Samuel, 53
Piper, John, 114
Pitt, Percy, 97, 104
Planché, J.R., 42, 66
Playfair, Nigel, 105
Plisetskaya, Maya, 81
Plunkett, Adeline, 64
Polish Ballet, 73
Ponomaryeva, Nina, 79
Ponselle, Rosa, 106
Ponsonby, 22
Powell, Claire, pl.46
Preobrazhenska, Olga, 67
Prêtre, Georges, pl.46; 121
Pritchard, Hannah, 45
Pritchard, John, pl.43; 110, 111
Prokhorova, Violetta see Elvin, Violetta
Promenade concerts (Proms), 101, 102, 113, 118
Pugin, Augustus Welby Northmore, 20
Pyne-Harrison Company, 103

Queen's Theatre, Haymarket, 21
Quick, John, 46
Quin, James, 41-5

Rainforth, Elizabeth, 94
Rambert, Dame Marie, 70
Rankl, Karl, 109, 111, 112, 117
Rassine, Alexis, 75
Reich, Günter, 119
Reiner, Fritz, 107
Reinhardt, Delia, 105, 106
Reinhardt, Max, 56, 116
Renault, Michel, 78
Rencher, Derek, pl.31; 87
Reynolds, Sir Joshua, 44
Riabouchinska, Tatiana, 72-3, 75-6
Ribbentrop, Joachim von, 107
Ricciarelli, Katia, pl.48
Rich, Christopher, 11, 41
Rich, John, pl.8; and first theatre, 11-14, 91; death, 15;
    career and acting, 41-3, 49, 60, 63; and
    Peg Woffington, 44; and George III's coronation, 45-6;
    inherits Handel's organ, 50, 93; and pantomime, 60;
    and dance, 63
Richards, John Inigo, 15
Richter, Hans, 97, 98, 103
Ricordi (music publishers), 105
riots: 1763, 13, 92, 93; 1809 ('OP'), 20, 50-1; Fitzpatrick
    and, 46; and Madame Vestris, 54
Robbins, Jerome, 75, 85, 89
Robinson, Forbes, pl.42
Rooy, Anton Van, 40

Rossi, J.C., 16, 28
Rossini, Gioacchino Antonio: *Semiramide*, 22
Rothschild, House of, 56
Rouleau, Joseph, pl.37
Royal Ballet School, 80-1, 82, 90
Royal Danish Ballet, 78, 80
Royal English Opera Company Ltd., 103
Royal (Italian) Opera Company, Covent Garden, 21-2, 39, 64, 91, 94-7, 111
Royal Opera House: name adopted, 97
Royal Opera House Company (1933), 36
Rubini, Giovanni Battista, 95
Rubinstein, Ida, 71, 72
Rundgren, Bengt, 118

Sabata, Victor de, 110
Sachs, Edwin O., 29, 35
Saint Léon, Arthur, 66
Sallé, Marie, 63
Saltzmann-Stevens, Minnie, 98
Samsova, Galina, pl.24
Sanjust, Filippo, pl.48; 117, 120
Schlesinger, John, pl.46; 121
Schöffler, Paul, 109
Schorr, Friedrich, 106
Schröder-Devrient, Wilhelmine, 95
Schumann, Elisabeth, 105, 106, 113
Schwarzkopf, Elisabeth, 109, 113
Scott, Sir Walter, pl.16; 20, 48
Scotti, Antonio, 101
Scotto, Renata, 121
Senesino (i.e. Francesco Bernardi), 91
Seymour, Lynn, 81, 82, 83, 86, 89
Shabelevsky, Yurek, 72
Shacklock, Constance, 116
Shaw, (Captain) Sir Eyre Massey, 34
Shaw, Brian, 78
Shearer, Moira, 75, 76
Shepherd, Edward, pl. 1; 11-14, 42
Sheridan, Richard Brinsley, 15, 47-8, 50
Shuard, Amy, pl.37; 111
Shuter, Edward, 46
Sibley, Antoinette, pl.31; 80-1, 82, 89
Siddons, Sarah, 47-8, 49, 51, 91
Siddons, William, 47-8
Silveri, Paolo, 109
Sizova, Alla, 79, 81
Skating Times, The, 74
Sleeping Beauty, The (ballet): 1946 performance, pl.20; 36, 73, 75, 77, 108
Sloman, Henry, 32
Smirke, Sir Robert, pl. 2, 3; 15-20, 23, 27-9, 31, 50, 93
Sokolova, Lydia, 69
Solovyov, Yury, 79, 81
Solti, Sir Georg, pl.41, 42; 111, 112, 113, 116
Somes, Michael, 78, 79, 81, 90
Spessivtseva, Olga, 69
Stabile, Mariano, 106
Stade, Frederica von, 114
Stanfield, 54
Stoll Theatre, 67
Strada de Po, Anna, 92
Strauss, Johann, 103
Strauss, Richard, pl.41; 103-5, 107, 117
Strehler, Giorgio, 119
Struchkova, Raissa, 81
Stuttgart Ballet, 88
subsidies, 107
Summers, Jonathan, pl.45
Supervia, Conchita, 107, 108
Sussex, Augustus Frederick, Duke of, 54
Sutherland, Dame Joan, pl.36; 110, 111, 119
Svoboda, Josef, pl.41
Szarvasy, F.A., 107

Taglioni, Filippo, 64
Taglioni, Marie, pl.17; 64
Taglioni, Paul, 64
Tamburini, Antonio, 95-6, 98
Tauber, Richard, 103, 107
Tchernicheva, Lubov, pl.32; 72, 75
Tear, Robert, 113, 116, 118
Tebaldi, Renata, 110
Tenducci, Giusto Ferdinando, 93
Terwesten, Augustyn, 30
Tetley, Glen, 85, 89
Tetrazzini, Luisa, 97
Theatres Act (1843), 55, 56
Thomas, W. Freeman, 101
Tippett, Michael, 110
Toms, Carl, pl.41; 39
Tooley, Sir John, 86, 113
Toscanini, Arturo, 105-6
Toumanova, Tamara, 72, 76
Tourel, Jennie, 116
Toye, Francis, 107
Toye, Geoffrey, 107
Turner, Dame Eva, 106, 107

Ulanova, Galina, 79, 81
Usher, Graham, 80, 82

Vanbrugh, Sir John, 12
Veasey, Josephine, pl.44; 118
Verardi, Signor, 22
Verdy, Violette, 84
Verrett, Shirley, pl.45
Vestris, Lucia Elizabeth, 20, 54-5
Vickers, Jon, pl.38, 45; 111, 113, 115, 119
Victoria, Queen, 22, 39, 54
Vieille Garde, La (group), 96
Vienna Philharmonic orchestra, 116
Vienna State Opera Company, 109
Vinay, Ramon, 110
Vining, Mrs, 65
Visconti, Luchino, pl.38; 113, 116, 117, 120

Wagner, Richard, 96, 97, 105, 115
Walker, David, pl.47
Walker, Edyth, 104
Walker, Norman, 116
Walker, Thomas, 42
Walmann, Margherita, pl.37
Wall, David, pl.31; 80, 86, 89
Walpole, Sir Robert, 1st Earl of Orford, 43
Walter, Bruno, 104, 105, 106-7, 116
Weber, Carl Maria von, 19, 93, 94-5
Weber, Ludwig, 109
Webster, Sir David, 79, 86, 109, 111
Weidemann, Hermann, 104
Weingartner, Felix, 107
Welitsch, Ljuba, 109, 117
Wells, Doreen, 80, 82
West, Christopher, 110
Whistler, Rex, 39
Whitten, Rosalyn, 85
Woffington, Margaret (Peg), 43-4, 91
Woizikowski, Leon, 69, 72
Woodward, Henry, 45
Wren, Sir Christopher, 12
Wright, Belinda, 80
Wright, Peter, pl.24; 80, 86, 90
Wyatt, Benjamin, 20

Yakar, Rachel, 118
Young, Cecilia, 91

Zarra, Monsieur, 22
Zeffirelli, Franco, pl.36; 116, 117
Zucchi, Virginia, 66